STUDENT'S BOOK AND WORKBOOK

with Digital Pack

COMBO B

3

CEFR B1+

CB077637

AMERICAN TH!NK

SECOND EDITION

Herbert Puchta,
Jeff Stranks &
Peter Lewis-Jones

CAMBRIDGE UNIVERSITY PRESS

CONTENTS

Intonation – inviting, accepting, and refusing invitations	**Train to THINK** Thinking outside the box **Values:** Stereotypes	**Reading** Article: Changing the rules Article: My prisoner, my friend, my president, and my father **Writing** An article about stereotypes **Listening** Conversation about traveling to India
Intonation – expressing surprise	**Train to THINK** Thinking about empathy **Values:** Respecting the law	**Reading** Newspaper articles: Crimes! Magazine article: Eating out behind bars **Writing** A report of a crime **Listening** Restoring Justice

TOWARDS B2 First for Schools practice

Moving word stress	**Train to THINK** Fact or opinion? **Values:** Thinking carefully before you act	**Reading** Web article: The truth is out there Magazine article: The dress **Writing** Explaining a mystery **Listening** A short story
Short and long vowel sounds: /ɪ/ – /iː/ and /ɑ/ – /oʊ/	**Train to THINK** Exaggeration	**Reading** Magazine article: Money: past, present, and future Web forum: Inequality **Writing** My life in the future **Listening** Game show: *Moneyspinners*

TOWARDS B2 First for Schools practice

Strong and weak forms: /tuː/ and /tə/	**Train to THINK** Understanding cause and effect	**Reading** News report: Miracle underground Article: Emergency? What emergency? **Writing** A story about a rescue **Listening** The story of *Androcles and the Lion*
Different pronunciations of *ea*	**Train to THINK** Logical conclusions **Values:** Breaking new ground	**Reading** Online forum: The first time I … A story: The first time I made friends with a spider **Writing** A story about a bad decision **Listening** Quiz: Transportation firsts

TOWARDS B2 First for Schools practice

7 BREAKING AWAY

OBJECTIVES

FUNCTIONS: talking about permission; talking about habits; invitations

GRAMMAR: *make / let* and *be allowed to; be / get used to*

VOCABULARY: phrasal verbs (1); personality; phrases with *all*

Get THINKING

Watch the video and think: who is the oldest person you know?

READING

1 **Look at the photos. What can you see? Use these words to help you.**

ironing | rugby | surfing

2 **Answer the questions.**

1 Do any of the photos make you laugh? If so, why?
2 Do you think any of the photos are strange? If so, why?
3 Do you think the photos have anything in common?

3 **Read the text that your teacher tells you to read (A or B). Answer the questions.**

1 Who is the text about?
2 In what way did the person do something different?
3 Who tried to stop the person from doing what they wanted to do?
4 Who (if anyone) helped the person?
5 What long-term effect did the person's actions have?

4 SPEAKING **Work in pairs. Using your answers to Exercise 3, tell your partner about your person.**

5 7.01 **Now read and listen to both texts. Answer the questions.**

1 How did Kathrine Switzer usually write her name?
2 What happened to Switzer after the race?
3 How much slower was Switzer 50 years later?
4 Why did Hogan not go to medical school?
5 Why did Hogan choose to go to MUW?
6 Why did MUW have to accept Hogan as a student?

Train to THINK

Thinking outside the box

In problem-solving, it can be useful to think really imaginatively, trying to avoid obvious or standard ideas. We call this "thinking outside the box." Sometimes thinking of very different possible answers to a problem helps us find the best solution.

It isn't a question of intelligence, just of thinking freely and creatively. The more you try it, the easier it is.

6 **Complete the table with as many ideas as you can think of.**

Questions about the texts	My "outside the box ideas"
1 Why did Semple want to stop Switzer?	*He wanted to get his photo in the newspaper.*
2 Why were a lot of women at MUW against letting Hogan in?	

7 **How many "outside the box" answers can you think of for these questions?**

1 What weighs more than it did half a year ago?
2 What are things money can't buy?
3 What can you do at school but not at home?

CHANGING THE RULES

A CHANGING THE MARATHON

In 1967, runner 261 was just one of hundreds of competitors in the Boston Marathon – K.V. Switzer. But something was different. The race started and soon spectators and photographers realized that K.V. Switzer was … a woman.

Back then, there was no rule that women couldn't run official long-distance races – they simply didn't and many thought they wouldn't want to. When Kathrine Switzer registered for the marathon, she wrote her initials as she always did, so no one found out she was a woman. When she showed up for the race, none of the race officials noticed, so when the starter fired the gun, she set off.

But after about six kilometers, an official named Jock Semple wanted to make her stop. He ran out, grabbed her, and tried to pull her off the road. Switzer's friend Tom Miller pushed Semple away and Switzer kept on running. She finished the race in 4 hours 20 minutes.

After the race, Switzer was banned from entering other competitions because she had run with men. However, newspaper reports of her run made many people question their ideas about women and running. In 1972, public opinion forced the organizers of the Boston Marathon to let women compete. One of them was Switzer. Later, she went on to play an important role as a campaigner, which led to the first ever women's Olympic marathon in the 1984 Games.

In 2017, Switzer ran the Boston Marathon again at age 70. She finished in 4 hours 44 minutes. And the organizers retired number 261 – no one will use that number again.

B A MALE STUDENT AT AN ALL-WOMEN'S COLLEGE

Joe Hogan took up nursing as a young man. He didn't have many qualifications, but he started working at a community hospital in Mississippi, US. In 1981, he decided that he wanted to get higher qualifications. He didn't have enough money to go to medical school, so he applied for a course in nursing. One option he had was to enroll at the University of Mississippi, but that was almost 200 km away from his home. He didn't want to move or to travel that far every day – so he applied to the Mississippi University for Women (MUW).

MUW leaders turned him down – as a college for women only, it did not allow men to study there. But Joe didn't give up. He went to court, but he lost the first time. He went to court again and in 1982, after a year of arguments, a panel of nine judges decided that MUW had to accept Joe as a student. The president of MUW (a man) was furious and many of the students (women) thought the decision was wrong and that the college should not let Hogan enroll. But the college, in the end, had no choice – and Hogan enrolled. MUW ended up accepting men in all its programs (not just nursing) and now a small number of men study there. The college has not changed its name, however.

SPEAKING

8 Work in pairs. Discuss these questions.

1 If you could meet either Switzer or Hogan, which one would you choose? What questions would you ask her or him?

2 Do you know any stories about someone who tried to change a situation they thought was wrong? Tell your partner.

GRAMMAR

make / let and *be allowed to*

1 **Complete these sentences from the texts on page 67. Then complete the rule with *make*, *let*, and *be allowed to*.**

1 Jock Semple wanted to ____________ her stop.
2 Newspaper reports of her run ____________ many people question their ideas.
3 Public opinion forced the organizers of the Boston Marathon to ____________ women compete.
4 As a college for women only, it ____________ men to study there.
5 Many of the students … thought … that the college should not ____________ Hogan enroll.

> **RULE:** We can use [6]______ *(someone do something)* and [7]______ to talk about permission. We can use [8]______ *(someone do something)* to talk about forcing someone to do something that they don't really want to do.

2 **Rewrite the sentences. Use each of the three structures at least once.**

0 I have to study every night. Dad says so.
Dad makes me study every night.
1 We can't eat food in the classroom.
____
2 I can sleep in on Sundays. My parents say so.
____
3 We have to read a book every week. The teacher says so.
____
4 I can listen to music in my bedroom. My dad says so.
____
5 We can wear our own clothes. The school says so.
____
6 We can't play soccer in the yard. Mom says so.
____
7 I don't have to go to bed early on Saturday. My parents say so.
____

→ workbook page 64

VOCABULARY

Phrasal verbs (1)

3 **Look at the underlined phrasal verbs in the texts on page 67. Match them with the definitions.**

1 began a journey
2 finally was in a situation or place (after some time or effort)
3 continued, didn't stop
4 started doing (a new activity)
5 got information or learned about (something new)
6 arrived or appeared at a place (usually late or unexpectedly)
7 quit (doing something)
8 refused, said "no" (to someone or something)

> **Look**
> The verbs in Exercise 3 are examples of phrasal verbs. These are usually formed with an ordinary verb (for example, *take*) and a particle (for example, *up*): *take up*. Together, they have a meaning that is often very different from the meaning of the verb alone.

4 **Underline the phrasal verbs in the sentences.**

1 I can't come tonight – I have to take care of my little brother at home.
2 Do you know what time the plane takes off tomorrow?
3 I had fun last night – my friends came over and we watched a movie.
4 She likes to hang out with her friends at the shopping mall.

5 **Complete the sentences with phrasal verbs from Exercises 3 and 4. Use the correct forms of the verbs.**

1 When we go on vacation, my friend ____________ my pet rabbit.
2 They offered Mom a job, but it was too far away, so she ____________ it ____________ .
3 She said she'd meet me at six o'clock, but she didn't ____________ until seven.
4 Would you like to ____________ to my house tonight?
5 I started learning Russian, but it was very difficult, so I ____________ after six months.
6 I don't know what her name is, but I'm going to ____________ !
7 She hurt her foot, but she ____________ playing until the end of the game.
8 I need to do more exercise, so I'm going to ____________ running and cycling.

→ workbook page 66

LISTENING

6 7.02 **Listen to a speaker talking to some students about his trip to India. Which of the things in the photos does he mention?**

A

B

C

7 7.02 **Listen again. Mark the sentences T (true) or F (false).**

According to the speaker, ...

1 he loved India immediately. ☐
2 India is a good place for people who don't eat meat. ☐
3 his Hindi is not very good. ☐
4 you need an open mind when you go abroad. ☐
5 everyone in a country is the same. ☐

WordWise: Phrases with *all*

8 Complete these sentences from the listening with the expressions.

all the time | after all | all the same | first of all

1 I mean, ________________, people are people – there are a variety of people all over the world.
2 Did you have to eat spicy food ________________?
3 So, ________________ I want to say that I think traveling is a great thing.
4 People aren't used to seeing foreigners. ________________, I thought everyone was really warm and kind.

9 Replace the underlined phrases with expressions from Exercise 8.

1 In England, it seems like it rains <u>every day</u>.
2 Welcome, everybody! <u>To begin</u>, I'd like to introduce myself.
3 Of course I like Italian food – <u>as an example to prove my point</u>, I eat pasta, don't I?
4 I know you don't like dentists. <u>Nevertheless</u>, if you're in pain, you should go and see one.

→ workbook page 66

GRAMMAR
be / get used to

10 Complete these sentences from the listening. Use the phrases in the list. Then complete the rule with *infinitive* or *gerund*.

aren't used to | 'm used to
gotten used to | get used to

1 I ________________ exploring and meeting new people.
2 In some places, people ________________ seeing foreigners.
3 I can't ________________ spicy food.
4 The trains are very crowded, but I soon ________________ that.

RULE: ***be / get used to*** is followed by a noun or noun phrase, or by a verb in the [5] ______ form. We use ***be / get used to*** (***doing***) ***something*** to talk about experiences and habits.

Look

Be used to refers to a state – something that is normal or familiar. ***Get used to*** refers to a process – something unusual *becomes* normal or familiar.

11 João is Brazilian, but he's living in London. Complete the sentences with the words.

British money | coats and sweaters
different accents | going | looking | speaking
sunshine | ~~traffic~~ | wearing | weather

0 I'm from Rio, so I'm used to *traffic*, but I'm not used to ________________ right before I cross the street!
1 I haven't gotten used to the ________________ yet. It rains a lot here. In Brazil, I was used to ________________.
2 It's hard to get used to all the ________________! I'm not used to ________________ so many clothes.
3 I'm used to ________________ now. But most stores close at 5:30. I'm not used to ________________ home so early.
4 I was used to ________________ English before I arrived. But I'll never get used to all the ________________ here.

→ workbook page 65

READING

1 **Look at the photos and the title. What do you think the article is about?**

A two men who built a prison
B a man whose father went to prison and became president
C a friendship between a prisoner and a prison warden
D a friendship between two prisoners

2 **Read the article quickly. Check your answer to Exercise 1.**

3 7.03 **Read the article again. At each point 1–6, choose the best answer. Then listen to check your answers.**

4 **Answer the questions.**

1 Where did Brand spend his childhood?
2 What kind of prisoners was Brand told he was going to work with?
3 What did Brand and Mandela have in common?
4 Why did Mandela and Brand have to keep their friendship secret?
5 What did Mandela do for Brand when he became president?

MY PRISONER, MY FRIEND,
MY PRESIDENT, AND MY FATHER

In 1978, Christo Brand joined the prison service. He was an 18-year-old white South African boy who had grown up on a farm. Now he was being sent to work as a warden in the famous prison on Robben Island. There, he was told he was going to work with the biggest criminals in South African history, including political prisoners. Brand didn't know very much about [1]*politics / prisoners* – he just knew that he was going to work with some dangerous people.

And then he met prisoner 46664, a quiet 60-year-old black man who started to talk to Brand and ask him questions – questions about his family, his education, his plans for the [2]*future / prison*. Prisoner 46664 was Nelson Mandela, who would one day become the first black president of South Africa.

"There was no [3]*language / color* barrier between us," said Brand, who later worked as a guide showing tourists around Robben Island. "Like me, Mandela came from a farm. We understood that we shared the same sky and the same air." The two men got along well and became really close, although this wasn't allowed by the prison authorities. They had to keep their friendship secret and their conversations had to be [4]*short / fascinating*. Brand found that Mandela was a warm and thoughtful person, even a little shy sometimes.

Mandela was also a generous man and he never forgot his friend. When he became president, he got Brand a job. One day, at a meeting of important politicians, Brand was in the room and was putting documents on the table. When Mandela came in, he saw Brand, went to him and hugged him. Mandela looked at [5]*Brand / all the people in the room* and said, "This person was my warden. This person was my [6]*friend / teacher*." Brand says that he felt very proud at that moment.

Nelson Mandela died in December of 2013, at age 95. Like so many people around the world, Brand was very sad when he heard the news. He said at the time, "Mandela was my prisoner, my friend, my president, and my father."

VOCABULARY
Personality

5 **Read the sentences about the listening on page 69 and the article on page 70. Choose the correct words.**

1 Everyone in India was *shy and rude* / *warm and kind*, even when we didn't understand each other well.
2 Some people can be *cold and unfriendly* / *lively and polite*, but everyone I met was really nice.
3 The writer describes Mandela as a *lively and selfish* / *generous and thoughtful* man.

6 **Which adjectives in Exercise 5 are positive, negative, and neutral? Mark them +, –, or 0. Use a dictionary to check the meaning of any of the words that you are unsure of.**

7 **Which adjectives describe each person? You can choose more than one for each person.**

1 *No, it's mine. You can't use it.*

2 *I don't want to go to the party, thanks. I'm not comfortable with strangers.*

3 *Jack got some bad news. Let's go and talk to him. Perhaps he needs a friend.*

4 *Don't worry. There's a problem, but everything's going to be all right, OK?*

5 *Go away! I'm working. I don't want to talk to you now.*

8 **Complete each response with an adjective. There may be more than one possible answer.**

1 A Hey, you! Get out of my way!
B What a ______ boy!
2 A The children aren't tired at all.
B Yes, they're very ______ tonight.
3 A Let's all go and have a hamburger. I'll pay.
B Wow! That's very ______ of you.
4 A He always says "please" and "thank you."
B Yes, he's very ______ .
5 A She never laughs or cries or anything.
B I know. She's a bit ______ sometimes.
6 A Mandy always thinks about other people.
B Yes, she's a really ______ person.

9 **Write four sentences about people you know. (You don't need to use their names!) Use adjectives from Exercise 5 and give reasons.**

I know someone who I think is rude because he/she never says hello at the bus stop.

10 SPEAKING **Compare your sentences with the class.**

→ workbook page 66

THINK values
Stereotypes

11 SPEAKING **Work in small groups. Discuss these questions.**

1 Think about your own country, or a region of your country. Do people from other places have fixed ideas about the people who live there?

Some people think the British are very polite but not very friendly.

2 Why do you think people have these ideas?
3 Do you think there is any truth in the stereotypes of your country or region?

12 **Some stereotypes are about nationalities. What other groups of people are there stereotypes about? Write a list. Then compare your ideas.**

People who live in small towns …

13 SPEAKING **In your groups, discuss stereotypes that you think people have about teenagers.**

WRITING
An article about stereotypes

14 **Write an article (80–120 words) for a school magazine about a national stereotype. Think about:**

- a culture that some people in your country see as a stereotype.
  In Britain, a lot of people think that Americans talk very loudly, only eat fast food, and wear colorful clothes.
- why you think the stereotype exists.
  I think it's because some American tourists in Britain are like that sometimes, and in some movies, too.
- why this stereotype is wrong.
  My friend went to the US last year. She said she ate excellent food and the Americans she met were quiet and fashionably dressed!

DEVELOPING SPEAKING

1 🔊 7.04 **Look at the photo. How do you think the people feel about each other? Listen and read to check.**

Jackie: Well, I think you're being unfair. Just because he likes different music than you do…

Luke: It's not just that and you know it! Harry's boring and there's no way I want him there.

Mom: Give it a rest, you two. Please! I'm tired of this endless arguing. What is it now? Let me guess. That's who you're going to invite.

Jackie: Well yeah, Mom. The thing is, we don't have the same friends, so it's hard when we're having just one party!

Luke: I'm with Jackie on this one, Mom. Can't we have two parties?

Mom: How is that going to work? You're twins, so your birthdays are on the same day. And we live in one house. One house, one day, one party. You can invite thirty people – end of story.

Jackie: So, Luke, we have to find a way to do this. Don't get me wrong, but I think you could be more … well, flexible, you know? I know you don't like Harry, but can't you get along with him for one evening?

Mom: Good point, Jackie.

Luke: Well, I suppose you're right.

Jackie: And listen, I promise you can invite Mary Tanner and I won't complain. OK?

Mom: That's more like it. A little bit of give-and-take.

Luke: Thanks for helping us sort it out, Mom.

Mom: Don't mention it. Now, let's all go out and buy some decorations.

2 🔊 7.04 **Listen and read the dialogue again. Answer the questions.**

1 Why can't Luke and Jackie have separate parties?
2 What does Jackie say Luke should try to do?
3 How does Jackie feel about Mary Tanner?
4 Who is going to buy decorations?

3 SPEAKING **Discuss the statements in pairs. What do you think?**

1 Luke and Jackie should have their parties on two different days.
2 Jackie's right to ask Luke to be nice to Harry.
3 Their mother sorts out their problem.

Phrases for fluency

4 **Find the underlined expressions in the dialogue. How do you say them in your language?**

5 **Replace each underlined part with an expression from the dialogue.**

1 A Thanks for your help.
  B You're welcome.
2 A If we don't leave now, we'll be late.
  B Yes, I think you're right. Let's go!
3 A You look happy. Good exam results?
  B Yes, of course I did! I got 95%.
4 A Dad, Alex won't let me use the computer.
  B Arguing again? Stop it now, before I get angry!
5 A You're always looking at your phone. Don't be offended, but I think you should use it less.
6 A It's raining. I suggest we watch a movie inside.
  B I agree with you. Which movie should we watch?

FUNCTIONS
Invitations

KEY LANGUAGE

Making invitations
Why don't you (join us)? / How about (coming with us)? Do you want to (go to the movies with me)?

Accepting invitations
That'd be (great). / I'd love to. / Yes, of course, thank you.

Declining an invitation
Sorry, I can't. / You'll have to count me out.

6 **Complete the sentences with the words in the list.**

about | count | course
don't | want | love | would

1 Why __________ you come along?
2 How __________ bringing some friends along with you?
3 Do you __________ to come along?
4 That __________ be fantastic.
  I'd __________ to.
5 Yes, of __________. It's a great idea.
6 You'll have to __________ me out.

ROLE PLAY **Work in pairs. Student A: turn to page 127. Student B: turn to page 128.**

PRONUNCIATION
Intonation – inviting, accepting, and refusing invitations Go to page 121.

LIFE COMPETENCIES

Getting along with others is important. We don't always agree with other people or like the way they do things. However, even when we disagree with them, we ought to be friendly and respect them.

1 ▶ 19 **Watch the vlog. How would you describe the situation at home between Leo and his sister?**

2 ▶ 19 **Watch the vlog again and make notes on:**

a three annoying things Leo does.

b three annoying things his sister does.

3 **Compare your notes with a partner.**

4 **Read the situations. Make notes about what you would do in each situation.**

A You are working on a project with a group of students in your class. You have a lot of good ideas that you want to use, but one person is difficult to work with. She also has lots of ideas for the project, but the problem is you don't think her ideas are very good. She says that you are too bossy and that you won't listen to anyone else, because you think your ideas are the best.

B You have always been good at English, particularly in creative writing, and you usually get good grades. You used to have a good relationship with your teacher, but recently, he has started to be pretty negative about your work and has even criticized it in front of the class. Last week, you got a really bad grade on your homework and you don't know why. When you tried to speak to your teacher about it, he seemed annoyed.

5 **Compare your answers with a partner. Do you agree? Have you ever been in a similar situation? What did you do?**

6 SPEAKING **Work in pairs. Match the solutions 1–4 to situations A and B in Exercise 4. Then discuss. Which solutions do you think are the best? Which would you *not* recommend?**

1 Suggest everyone in the group votes on which ideas to use. Both of you will have to be prepared to accept that it may not be your ideas that are chosen.

2 Confront your teacher again and ask for an explanation. Explain that your work won't improve unless he gives you clear feedback on exactly what the problem is. Refuse to leave until it is resolved.

3 Listen to your friend's ideas and think about how they could work with your own. Maybe you could use some of your ideas and some of hers, too.

4 Try talking to another teacher. Ask him/her for advice on how to deal with the situation.

Me and my world

7 **Think of someone you don't get along well with. Write down:**

1 three reasons why you don't get along.

2 three things you could do to change things.

TIPS FOR GETTING ALONG WITH OTHERS

- Take a bit of time to stop and think about what someone has said or done. Don't respond or react in anger. This could make the situation worse.
- Be positive. Think of solutions to your problem before you speak to the person.
- Try to feel empathy. There may be a reason why the person is behaving a certain way. Ask how they are feeling.

8 CRIME AND PUNISHMENT

OBJECTIVES

FUNCTIONS: reporting what someone said, asked, or requested; giving and reacting to news

GRAMMAR: reported speech (review); reported questions, requests, and imperatives

VOCABULARY: crime; reporting verbs

Get THINKING

Watch the video and think:
do you always pay for the music you listen to?

A

D

B

E

C

F

READING

1 **Look at the words for different types of criminals. How do you say them in your language?**

1 burglar
2 con artist
3 poacher
4 pickpocket
5 bank robber
6 shoplifter

2 **Match the pictures with words from Exercise 1.**

3 **Think of examples of these criminals from the news, books, TV, or movies.**

4 8.01 **Look at the photos and headlines on the next page. Guess what the news stories are about. Then read and listen to check.**

5 **Read the news stories again. In which stories do these things happen? Write *lion* or *rhino*.**

1 The criminals tried to get rid of the evidence. ______
2 The criminals were caught as they tried to kill the animal. ______
3 The criminals attacked the agents. ______
4 The criminals were caught after a car chase. ______
5 It was not the first time the criminals had gotten into trouble. ______
6 The agents found important evidence among the criminals' possessions. ______
7 The criminals are facing charges for three different crimes. ______
8 Agents believe their work is starting to make a difference. ______

Train to THINK

Thinking about empathy

To understand another person's feelings, you need to "put yourself in their shoes" – try to imagine how you'd feel in their situation.

6 **Read the first story again. Who do you think felt these emotions? Match 1–2 with a–b.**

1 the agents ☐
2 the poachers ☐

a excitement and pride
b regret and guilt

7 **Why do you think they might have felt these things? What other emotions do you think they might feel?**

8 **How do these stories make you feel? Tell your partner.**

CRIMES!

POACHERS *ARRESTED*

Anti-poaching agents in Limpopo, South Africa caught two poachers as they tried to kill lions at the Letaba River Wildlife Reserve Park last Sunday evening.

The agents had received information about the planned attack and made plans of their own to catch the criminals in the act.

Under a full moon, the poachers broke into the park where the agents were waiting. They jumped on the poachers as they approached the cages where the lions were kept for their own protection. After a short fight in which one of the poachers used a knife, the agents were able to arrest the two men.

One of the agents said that they had searched the men's bags and had found poisoned dead chickens and wire cutting equipment. He explained how poachers throw the chickens to the lions, wait for the lions to eat the chickens, and then return when the animals are dead. He also said that the poachers could sell the dead animals for over $3,500.

The poachers are now in jail awaiting trial. The prisoners are facing charges of attempted poaching, possession of a dangerous weapon, and attempted murder. If found guilty, they could go to prison for up to ten years. An anti-poaching agent said he hoped this would be a warning to other poachers and help in their fight against one of their country's most serious problems.

CAUGHT *RED-HANDED*

In another part of Limpopo, three rhino horn smugglers have been caught red-handed by members of the Limpopo Endangered Species Unit. The agents had received information the men were trying to sell the illegal item. As they approached the men's car, it drove away quickly and a large item was thrown from the window. While one agent got the item, which turned out to be the horn, others chased and caught the three men. Two of the men, who are brothers, were already known to the agents. They had been arrested in 2014 for rhino poaching but had not been sent to prison and were let go. This time agents are hoping they will finally be sent to prison. They believe the horn comes from a rhino that was shot dead a week ago in a nearby area. Agents said they were going to send the horn for testing to see if they are right.

Rhino poaching continues to be a huge problem in many southern African countries as the demand for their horns increases around the world. But South African law officers are determined to protect the animals and are spending more money to catch those committing the crimes. An official from the department of environmental affairs said that the situation was improving and that the number of rhino deaths in 2016 had fallen since the record number of over 1,200 in 2014. They also said they are using modern technology in their fight. One technique is to put a dye into the rhino's horns, which is poisonous for humans but perfectly safe for the rhinos.

SPEAKING

9 SPEAKING **Work in pairs. Discuss these questions.**

1 What punishment do you think these men should get?

2 What other animals do you know that are in danger from poachers?

GRAMMAR
Reported speech (review)

1 **Complete the sentences with suitable verbs. Then check your answers in the news stories on page 75.**

1 One of the agents said that they ______________ the men's bags.
2 He also said the poachers ______________ the dead animals for over $3,500.
3 An anti-poaching agent said that he ______________ this ______________ be a warning to other poachers.
4 Agents said they ______________ the horn for testing.
5 An official from the department of environmental affairs said that the situation ______________ .
6 He said that the number of rhino deaths in 2016 ______________ since the record number of over 1,200 in 2014.

2 **Match what was said (direct speech) with the reported sentences in Exercise 1. <u>Underline</u> the verb forms which are different. Then complete the rule.**

a "We're going to send the horn for testing."
b "I hope this will be a warning to other poachers."
c "The number of rhino deaths in 2016 has fallen since the record number of over 1,200 in 2014."
d "The poachers can sell the dead animals for over $3,500."
e "We searched their bags."
f "The situation is improving."

RULE:

Direct speech		**Reported speech**
simple present	→	0 *simple past*
present continuous	→	1 ______________
present perfect	→	2 ______________
simple past	→	3 ______________
past perfect	→	*past perfect*
would	→	*would*
can	→	4 ______________
will	→	5 ______________
am/ is / are going to	→	6 ______________

3 **Rewrite these sentences in reported speech.**

1 "I'll be happy to put cameras all over the park," the manager said.
2 "The agents can't wait for the DNA report," the reporter said.
3 "We saw the men from across the street," the woman told the police.
4 "We're thinking of having a new alarm installed," the manager said.
5 "We haven't done anything," one of the brothers said.
6 "You'll get a long time in jail for this," the agent told the poachers.

→ workbook page 72

VOCABULARY
Crime

4 **Match the words with the definitions.**

murder | break in | arrest | a fine
commit a crime | go to prison | a murderer
get into trouble | get caught | a prisoner

1 to do something illegal
2 to be made to live in a special building for criminals
3 to take (a suspected criminal) to the police station
4 to kill (a person) intentionally
5 money that you have to pay if you break a law
6 to enter by force (usually to steal something)
7 someone who intentionally kills another person
8 to be found while committing a crime
9 to have a problem because of something that you did wrong
10 a person who is in prison

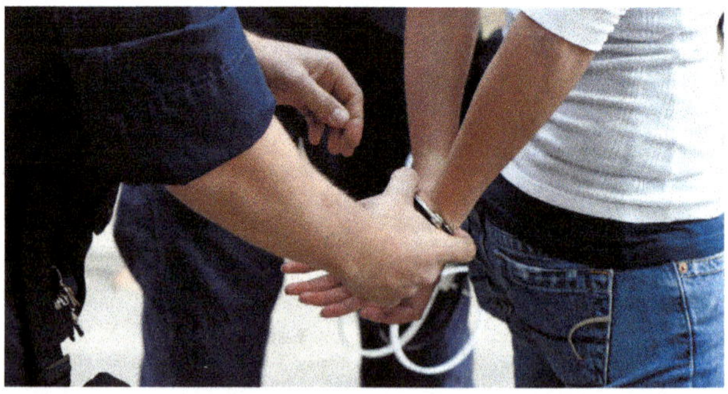

5 SPEAKING **Work in pairs. Use these questions to help you invent a crime story. Make notes and then tell your partner your story.**

- Where and when did it happen?
- Who was involved?
- What happened?
- What crime was committed?
- How did the police react?
- What happened to the criminal?

→ workbook page 74

LISTENING

6 SPEAKING **Imagine a young person mugged somebody. Discuss these questions.**

1 Why might someone mug a person?
2 Who might suffer as a result?
3 What would be the best punishment?

7 8.02 **Listen to a radio interview. What is Restoring Justice and who is it for?**

8 8.02 **Listen again and make notes on these topics.**

1 Jason's initial reaction to Restoring Justice
2 the main idea behind Restoring Justice
3 how Jason felt about meeting his victim
4 how Mrs. Schwartz felt about meeting her mugger
5 the reason Jason gave for mugging Mrs. Schwartz
6 the people Mrs. Schwartz feels suffered most

GRAMMAR

Reported questions, requests, and imperatives

9 **Match 1–4 with a–d. Then complete the rule with *asked*, *if*, *told*, and *whether*.**

1 She asked me if I knew who'd suffered ☐
2 [The judge] asked me whether I wanted ☐
3 [She] asked me to look at the other side ☐
4 He told me to ☐

a think carefully about my choices.
b to go to prison.
c of the table, where my mom and dad were sitting.
d most from what I'd done.

RULE:
- In reported *yes / no* questions, we use *asked* + [5] ______ or ______ and the same word order as in a statement.
- In reported requests, we use [6] ______ + object + infinitive with *to*.
- In reported imperatives, we use [7] ______ + object + infinitive with *to*.

10 **These are things people have said to Ken, the social worker. Rewrite them in reported speech.**

0 Reporter: "Have you had much success with the program so far?"
The reporter asked if he'd had much success with the program so far.
1 Reporter: "Are victims scared of meeting their muggers?"
2 Ken's wife: "Did you see the article about Restoring Justice in the newspaper this morning?"
3 Reporter: "Could you tell us more about the ideas behind the program, please?"
4 Ken's manager: "Don't include other criminals in the program."

11 **Write four to six more questions that Mrs. Schwartz might ask Jason. Use direct speech. Then put your partner's questions into reported speech.**

"How do you see your future?"
She asked him how he saw his future.

→ workbook page 72

TH!NK values

Respecting the law

12 **Match the punishments (1–6) with the sentences (a–f).**

1 He got a fine. ☐
2 He got community service. ☐
3 He got a life sentence. ☐
4 He got a warning. ☐
5 He got the death penalty. ☐
6 He got a prison sentence. ☐

a He has to spend 80 hours cleaning the streets.
b But he'll be in serious trouble if he does it again.
c It means at least 20 years in prison.
d But it will be years before they carry it out.
e He had to pay $100.
f He'll be locked up for two years.

13 **Number the punishments in Exercise 12 from 1 (least serious) to 6 (most serious).**

14 SPEAKING **Work in pairs. Read these newspaper headlines. What crimes have been committed? What punishment (if any) would be fair?**

- Hungry student steals chocolate bar from store
- Man steals TV from old couple's home
- Speeding driver kills family of four
- Bank robber escapes with thousands

READING

1 Read the article quickly. What do these numbers refer to?

a 16% b 25% c 361 d 78 e 250

EATING OUT

BEHIND BARS

Next time you're looking for a special evening out, why not invite someone special to eat out with you at one of the Clink restaurants? They offer delicious, beautifully cooked dishes, but this is fine dining with a difference, because these are no ordinary restaurants. The Clink restaurants are found inside four of the UK's most famous prisons: High Down, Brixton, Cardiff, and Styal, so your waiter might be a burglar and your food might have been cooked by a robber. Because the restaurants are actually inside the prison walls, anyone wanting to eat out in one of the Clink prisons has to agree to go through a special security check first.

The man behind the idea is Chef Alberto Crisci, who was looking for a way to help prisoners make the most of their time inside by studying for professional cooking qualifications. He also wanted to offer members of the public a chance to eat out somewhere truly different, so he set up the Clink charity to make all this happen. The idea is to encourage prisoners to learn how to do a new job while they are in prison. When they are released from prison with their newly earned qualifications, they can persuade restaurant owners to give them a job. Many hope that then they will be less likely to commit crimes in the future.

Supporters of the restaurants claim that it really works. They explain that only 16% of prisoners who have worked in the Clink restaurants commit crimes in the year after they are released – compared to the national average of 25% of adult prisoners. Some critics refuse to accept these figures. They say that only the prisoners who are not likely to return to crime are chosen to work in the restaurants. But the organizers of the charity are not worried by this argument. They have plenty more evidence to show how successful they are. In 2018, 361 prisoners were trained in the Clink restaurants and 142 earned a professional qualification; 78 out of 112 ex-prisoners who had worked in Clink found jobs on release and 250 restaurants said they were happy to take on graduates from the training program. One graduate even made a successful appearance on the TV cooking show *Bake Off: The Professionals*.

So if you're looking for a great meal out and like the idea of helping a criminal make a new start, one of the Clink restaurants might just be the place you're looking for. But I'd recommend that you book early. The restaurants are extremely popular.

2 8.03 **Read and listen to the article and mark the sentences T (true) or F (false).**

1 The food in the Clink restaurants is not particularly good. ☐
2 Alberto Crisci wanted to improve the quality of meals in prisons. ☐
3 You can't just walk into a Clink restaurant. ☐
4 Prisoners with Clink qualifications are less likely than other prisoners to go back to prison. ☐
5 Not everyone agrees that the program is really successful. ☐
6 It's easy to get a table at one of the Clink restaurants. ☐

3 SPEAKING **Work in pairs. Discuss these questions.**

1 Would you like to visit a Clink restaurant? Why (not)?
2 What other useful skills could prisoners learn in prison?

VOCABULARY
Reporting verbs

4 Complete the sentences with the correct forms of the verbs. Then check your answers in the article on page 78.

agree | claim | encourage | explain | invite
persuade | recommend | refuse

1 Supporters of the restaurant ______ that it works.
2 They ______ that only 16% of prisoners who have worked in the Clink restaurants commit crimes in the year after they are released.
3 Anyone wanting to eat out in one of the Clink prisons has to ______ to go through a special security check first.
4 Why not ______ someone special to eat out with you at one of the Clink restaurants?
5 I'd ______ that you book early.
6 Some critics ______ to accept these figures.
7 The idea is to ______ prisoners to learn how to do a new job.
8 They can ______ restaurant owners to give them a job.

5 Match the verbs (1–5) with the definitions (a–e).

1 agree ☐
2 claim ☐
3 explain ☐
4 persuade ☐
5 refuse ☐

a make something clear
b try to get someone to do or believe something
c accept an idea or a suggestion
d say no
e say that something is true

6 Complete the rule with reporting verbs from Exercises 4 and 5. Some verbs can go in more than one list.

RULE:
We use different structures with different reporting verbs.
1 verb + (*not*) infinitive with *agree, offer*, ______, ______
2 verb + object + (*not*) infinitive with *ask, tell*, ______, ______, ______
3 verb + *that* + clause: *say, claim*, ______, ______, ______
4 verb + gerund: *apologize for, suggest*, ______

7 Complete the sentences with the correct forms of the verbs and any other necessary words.

1 Liam agreed ______ (meet) me at nine o'clock.
2 Lucy apologized ______ (forget) my birthday.
3 Jack refused ______ (help) us.
4 Bobby persuaded ______ (me / go) to the party with him.
5 Dad suggested ______ (have) dinner at a restaurant.
6 My mom encouraged ______ (me / enter) the singing competition.
7 Mr. Jones recommended ______ (we / read) the book before we saw the movie.
8 Liz offered ______ (drive) me home after the game.

8 Rewrite the sentences in reported speech. Use suitable reporting verbs. Sometimes more than one verb is possible.

1 "We forgot to inform you. We're really sorry," they said.
2 "We're going to introduce a new system to reduce crime," the mayor said.
3 "Can you give us more information about the plan?" the reporter said to the official.
4 "If you work for us, you'll be very rich soon," the man said.
5 "I don't want to buy the watch because it's too expensive," the woman said.
6 "Study this text carefully!" the teacher said to the class.
7 "I can help you with your work," the man said.
8 "Come to my office tomorrow morning, please," the principal said to my parents.
9 "Oh, all right. I'll go to the movies with you, but only if you pay," Jack said to Olivia.

→ workbook page 74

WRITING
A report of a crime

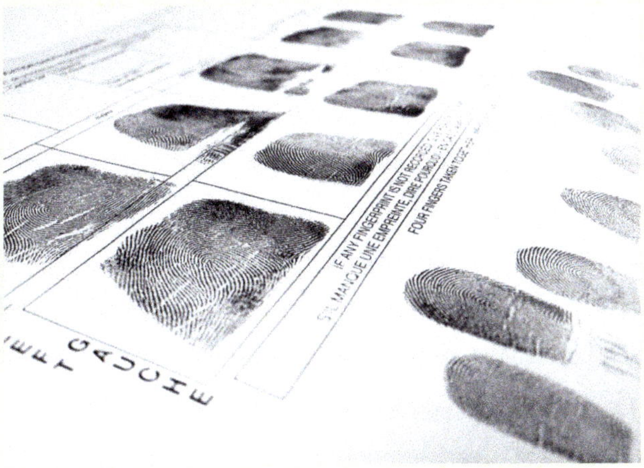

9 Write a newspaper report about a crime (100–150 words).

- Give a description of the crime (what happened).
- Include what one witness said.
- Say what the investigators think.

TH!NK

Famous prisons

Culture

1 **Scan the article and find one famous prisoner from each prison.**

2 8.04 **Read and listen to the article to check your answers.**

FAMOUS PRISONS

1 ROBBEN ISLAND, SOUTH AFRICA

Robben Island is known all over the world because of one of its **former** prisoners. From 1964 until 1982, this island prison, 11 km off the coast of Cape Town, was home to perhaps the most famous prisoner in the world, Nelson Mandela, who in 1994 became the first black president of his country. Robben Island was used mainly for political prisoners and more than 3,000 of them spent time there before it was finally closed in 1996. These days it is a museum and it is visited by thousands of tourists each year.

2 ALCATRAZ, US

Another island that was home to a prison is Alcatraz, which is situated 2 km off the coast of San Francisco. Probably America's most well-known prison, Alcatraz had many famous **inmates**, such as the gangster Al Capone and Robert "Birdman" Stroud, a murderer who was also one of the country's biggest **experts** on birds. Alcatraz closed in 1963 and in its 29 years of being a prison, no one ever escaped, although 36 prisoners tried. These days it is open to the public and tourists can take a short boat ride across the San Francisco Bay to visit it.

3 THE TOWER OF LONDON, UK

The Tower of London, which was built in the 11th century, is now one of the city's most popular tourist attractions, with people coming from all over the world to see the Crown **Jewels** that are kept inside it. However, up until the mid 20th century, it was a prison and home to many famous prisoners, including King Henry VI and two of King Henry VIII's wives, Anne Boleyn and Catherine Howard, who were also both **executed** in the Tower. Visitors see the **cells** and enjoy interactive displays that show what life was like in this ancient prison.

4 CHÂTEAU D'IF, FRANCE

Although Château d'If is a real island, most people know of it because of a fictional prisoner. The island prison, which is situated off the coast of Marseilles in the south of France, was home to many criminals from the mid 17th century to the end of the 19th century, but it is really famous for one prisoner who was never actually there. In his novel *The Count of Monte Cristo*, French author Alexandre Dumas tells the story of Edmond Dantès, an **innocent** man who is sent to the prison for a crime he did not commit. In the book, Dantès manages to escape, something that no prisoner was ever able to do in real life.

5 DEVIL'S ISLAND, FRENCH GUIANA

Devil's Island is off the coast of French Guiana in the Caribbean. For the hundred years that it was open, it was known as one of the toughest prisons in the world and fewer than 25% of all prisoners who went there left the island alive. The prison was set in the middle of a jungle and the waters around it were full of man-eating sharks, which made escape almost impossible. One man who managed to escape and write a book about his experiences was Henri Charrière and the movie *Papillon* tells his story. Since it was closed in 1953, Devil's Island has become a **tourist attraction** for passengers on the many cruise ships that pass nearby.

3 **Answer the questions.**

According to the texts, which prison or prisons …

1 was impossible to escape from?
2 was home to a future politician?
3 can now be visited by members of the public?
4 is not on an island?
5 contains really valuable objects?
6 appeared in a book?

4 SPEAKING **Work in pairs. Discuss these questions.**

1 What other famous prisons do you know of either in real life or in movies/books?
2 Would you like to visit any of these prisons? Why or why not?

5 VOCABULARY **There are eight highlighted words or phrases in the article. Match the words with these meanings. Write the words.**

1 rooms in prison where prisoners are kept
2 killed as a legal punishment
3 valuable stones
4 place visited by people on vacation
5 at an earlier time
6 people who know a lot about something
7 not guilty
8 people who are kept in prison

LISTENING

6 8.05 **Listen to the conversations and match them with the photos.**

A

B

C

D

7 8.05 **Listen again and complete the notes.**

Conversation 1

Criminal: ______ What was taken: ______

Conversation 2

Criminal: ______ What was taken: ______

Conversation 3

Criminal: ______ What was taken: ______

Conversation 4

Criminal: ______ What was taken: ______

FUNCTIONS

Giving and reacting to news

8 **Put the words in order to form expressions for giving news from the conversations.**

1 never / You'll / happened / what / guess
2 believe / won't / to / week / what / You / happened / last / me
3 about / a / really / an / sad / lady / story / heard / I / old
4 paper / a / scary / story / There / the / was / other / in / day / the

9 **Complete the reactions to news.**

1 T _ l l m _ .
2 W h _ t?
3 R _ _ l l y?
4 T h _ t's _ w f _ l!
5 N _ w _ y!

10 SPEAKING **Work in pairs. Make conversations using the expressions from Exercises 8 and 9.**

- Think of (or make up) a piece of news.
- Take turns to give your news.
- React and ask for more details.

PRONUNCIATION
Intonation – expressing surprise
Go to page 121.

READING AND USE OF ENGLISH

Word formation

→ workbook page 71

1 **For questions 1–7, read the text below. Use the word given in capitals at the end of some of the lines to form a word that fits in the gap in the same line. There is an example at the beginning (0).**

A thief who kissed his victim after a ⁰ *robbery* in a	**ROB**
French jewellery shop has been caught after a forensic	
¹__________ matched his DNA with that left on the	**SCIENCE**
hand of his victim.	
The thief ²__________ the Parisian shop late in the	**ENTRY**
afternoon, as the owner was preparing to close for the	
evening. After tying the woman to a chair, he smashed	
open ³__________ display cabinets and loaded	**VARY**
⁴__________ worth more than 20,000 euros into	**VALUE**
a bag. Before leaving the shop, he kissed the owner's	
hand and made an ⁵__________ for his crime.	**APOLOGISE**
However, the ⁶__________ thief could never have	**LUCK**
imagined that the kiss would lead to his arrest.	
Police used the DNA and ran it through a	
database of all known ⁷__________ .	**CRIME**

WRITING

An informal email

→ workbook page 79

2 **You have received an email from an English-speaking penfriend.**

To: Mike
mike_2000@mail.com

Subject: Any suggestions?

Hey Mike,
How are things? Listen, I'm writing because a friend of mine is coming to spend a few days in your town. She asked me to write to you to see if you could suggest some of the things she should do while she's there. She also wanted to know what the weather's like and what clothes she should bring with her. She leaves on Friday. Sorry for the short notice, but can you help?
Hope to hear from you soon.
Best,
Angie

Write your email in 140–190 words.

TEST YOURSELF UNITS 7 & 8

VOCABULARY

1 Complete the sentences with the words / phrases in the list. There are four extra words / phrases.

give up | got into trouble | unfriendly | generous | find out | after all
commit a crime | polite | selfish | set off | burglar | shy | arrested | end up

1 Don't ______________________ now. You're a great player. I'm sure you'll get on the team next time.
2 That was very ______________________ of you to eat all those cookies and not leave any for us.
3 We ______________________ very early in the morning because we wanted to arrive before it got dark.
4 Tim ______________________ for not doing his English homework again.
5 The ______________________ broke into the house when everybody was asleep.
6 I hope they ______________________ who stole Amanda's purse.
7 It was very ______________________ of James to pay for all your concert tickets.
8 It rained a lot that day, so we didn't go on the school trip ______________________ .
9 The police finally ______________________ the con man and he went to prison.
10 Emma's very ______________________ . She always says "please" and "thank you."

/10

GRAMMAR

2 Complete the sentences with the words / phrases in the list. There are two extra words / phrases.

get used to | would | 'm not used to | going to | encouraged | is | had been | gotten used to

1 My mom ______________________ me to do well in school.
2 The police officer told me that the robber ______________________ get a prison sentence.
3 I ______________________ taking my shoes off before I go into a house, but here in Japan, it's what everyone does.
4 She says she is ______________________ report the crime to the police.
5 At home, I always have dinner at six o'clock, so I haven't ______________________ eating at nine o'clock here in Spain.
6 She said the con artist ______________________ sentenced to two years in prison.

3 Find and correct the mistake in each sentence.

1 She asked me if I knew who has taken the bike.
2 My mom let me do all the dishes for a week because I was late home one night.
3 He persuaded me report the incident to the police.
4 I really want to go on the school trip, but my dad won't make me.
5 The reporter explained me that the mugger would get community service.
6 My parents make me to clean my bedroom.

/12

FUNCTIONAL LANGUAGE

4 Choose the correct words.

1 A We're going camping this weekend. Why don't you come *along* / *on*?
B I'd love to. How *for* / *about* asking Mike to come, too?
2 A We're going swimming. Does anyone *feel* / *want* to join us?
B You can *call* / *count* me out. I hate swimming.
3 A The other day, I *hear* / *heard* a really sad story about an old man whose house was broken into.
B *That's* / *It's* awful.
4 A You'll never *believe* / *understand* what happened to me last week!
B Go on. *Say* / *Tell* me!

/8

MY SCORE /30

22–30 | 10–21 | 0–9

9 IT'S A MYSTERY!

OBJECTIVES

FUNCTIONS: making deductions

GRAMMAR: modals of deduction (present); *should(n't) have*; modals of deduction (past)

VOCABULARY: mysteries; expressions with *go*

Get THINKING

Watch the video and think: are there any unexplained mysteries from your country?

A

C

B

D

READING

1 **Look at the photos and match them with the mysteries.**

1 Stonehenge | 2 the Loch Ness Monster
3 the yeti | 4 UFOs

2 SPEAKING **Work in pairs. Compare your answers. What do you know about these mysteries?**

3 **Read the article on the next page quickly. Why *isn't* the author writing about any of the mysteries in Exercise 1?**

4 9.01 **Read and listen to the article. Write Sp (spheres), O (octopuses), S (spaceman), or V (Voynich) in the boxes to answer the questions.**

Which mystery ...

1 is about the appearance of a mysterious character? ☐
2 is about things that were difficult to make? ☐
3 is a challenge to language experts? ☐
4 is about the unusual behavior of some creatures? ☐
5 involves huge stone objects? ☐
6 involves a book written centuries ago? ☐
7 can perhaps be explained by the weather? ☐
8 is about a family and a photograph? ☐

Train to THINK

Fact or opinion?

A fact is something that can be proven to be true. An opinion is a personal belief. It's important to be able to see the difference.

5 **Read about the octopuses again. According to what is written in the text, mark the sentences F (fact) or O (opinion).**

1 The population of the octopuses is bigger now than before. ☐
2 The octopuses needed to travel to find food. ☐
3 There were storms not long before they were seen walking on the beach. ☐
4 The octopuses had a disease. ☐

6 **Complete the table with two facts and two opinions for each mystery according to the article.**

	Facts	Opinions
1 Giant stone spheres		
2 Solway spaceman		
3 Voynich manuscript		

THE TRUTH IS OUT THERE

There are many unexplained mysteries in the world. How was the Great Pyramid at Giza built? Are there yetis in the Himalayas? Is there a monster in the depths of Loch Ness? Here are our favorites.

A The octopuses that walked on land

You might see an octopus hop from one rock pool to another, but in late October of 2017, more than 20 octopuses were seen coming out of the water and moving along a beach in Wales. "No one has ever seen anything like this before," said one local. "It's very odd behavior." So, why did it happen? Different experts have different opinions. One is that the octopuses were sick. Another is that two big storms a few days earlier had confused the octopuses and affected their senses. A third expert said, "There's been an increase in the octopus population, so perhaps the octopuses needed to travel further to find food."

B The giant stone spheres

There are hundreds of large stone spheres in the Costa Rican jungle. Evidence shows that they must be at least 600 years old and some could date back to 200 BCE. The objects are up to 2.4 meters in diameter and are almost perfectly round. They are also very heavy, with some of them weighing 16 tons. The stone itself comes from miles away, so it took a huge effort to move them. It's thought they probably had a religious purpose and some people suggest a connection with the sun. Others have even suggested that the spheres were created by an alien life form. But no one really knows and the mystery continues.

C The Solway spaceman

In 1964, Jim Templeton from Carlisle took a photo of his daughter Elizabeth and was surprised to see in the photo a strange figure behind her that looked like an extraterrestrial spaceman. Jim took the photo with the mysterious figure to the police, and soon afterwards it appeared in the newspapers. Then one day, Jim was visited by two men who said they were government officials. They asked him to take them to the scene of the photograph. Who were they? Why were they interested? Some people say the figure in the photo must be Templeton's wife – the camera flash made her dress look bright white. Most people agree that the image is real but can't be a spaceman. What do you think?

D The Voynich manuscript

In 1639, Georgius Barschius from Prague told a friend that he had a mysterious book that might be about science or medicine. It was full of puzzling pictures and diagrams, and it was written in an unknown language. Today, the Voynich manuscript is over 600 years old and still no one can read it. It has been suggested that the mysterious writing could be based on an Arabic or Roma or Aztec language. Others say it must be a secret code, and many expert codebreakers have tried to crack it. Every year people think they have solved the mystery, but no one ever has.

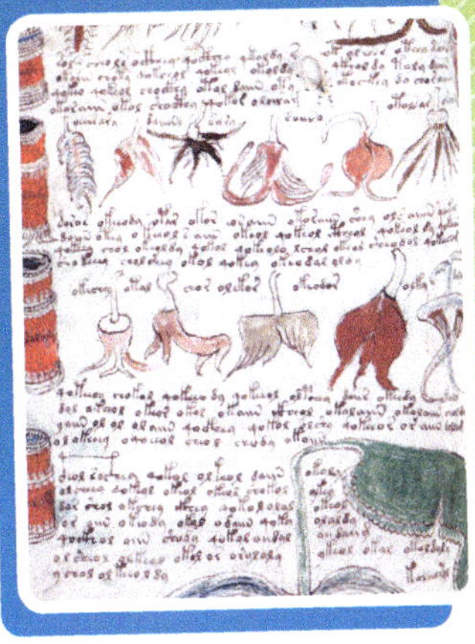

SPEAKING

7 Work in pairs. Discuss these questions.

1 Which of these mysteries do you think is the most interesting? Why?
2 What other mysteries do you know of?

PRONUNCIATION
Moving word stress Go to page 121.

GRAMMAR
Modals of deduction (present)

1 Complete the sentences from the article on page 85. Use *must, can't, could,* and *might*. Then complete the rule.

1 You ______ see an octopus hop from one rock pool to another.
2 Some of the giant stone spheres ______ date back to 200 BCE.
3 Most people agree that the image ______ be a spaceman.
4 Others say that it ______ be a secret code.

> **RULE:**
> When we're sure something is true, we use [5]______ .
> When we're sure something isn't true, we use [6]______ .
> When we think something is possibly true, but aren't sure, we use [7]______ or ______ .

2 Complete the sentences with suitable modal verbs. Sometimes there's more than one possible answer.

1 They're speaking Spanish, so they ______ be from Argentina, I suppose.
2 She ______ love cats – she has 20.
3 You ______ want more – you've already eaten two whole pizzas!
4 I'm not sure, but I think that man ______ need our help. I don't think he can swim.
5 You've been working all day. You ______ feel really tired.
6 He's a little older than John, but he ______ know him. I think they went to the same school.
7 Tim ______ be happy. He studied really hard, but he still failed the test.
8 It's the world's oldest mystery. You ______ know the answer.

→ workbook page 82

VOCABULARY
Mysteries

3 Add the missing vowels to make adjectives related to mysteries.

1 _ n _ x p l _ _ n _ d mysteries
2 _ d d behavior
3 _ l _ _ n life form
4 s t r _ n g _ figure
5 _ x t r _ t _ r r _ s t r _ _ l spaceman
6 m y s t _ r _ _ _ s writing
7 p _ z z l _ n g pictures
8 a s _ c r _ t code

4 Answer the questions about the words from Exercise 3.

1 Which two words mean "from another world"?
2 Which word means "known by very few people"?

5 Complete the text with the adjectives from Exercise 3.

I left for school at the usual time, but something seemed wrong. The streets were empty and there was a [1]m ______ feeling in the air. I passed a few people, but they all seemed rather [2]o ______ . I didn't see anyone from school on the way. When I got to school, the gates were closed. Why were they closed? I looked at my watch – 9 a.m. The gates should be open. This was extremely [3]p ______ .

I pushed the gates open and walked inside. Where was everyone? Had they been transported away by some [4]e ______ beings and taken to an [5]a ______ planet? Had they all been taken away as part of some [6]s ______ government experiment? What should I do? Run away? No, this was one mystery that couldn't be left [7]u ______ . I had to find out where everyone was.

I opened the school door and walked inside. I saw a man – it was Mr. Barnes, who looked after the school. I ran up to him. "Thank goodness!" I cried. "Where is everyone?" He gave me a [8]s ______ look.

"At home, probably," he replied. "It's Saturday morning."

→ workbook page 84

LISTENING

6 Match the pictures with the words.

A

B

C

D

1 fortune teller 2 rope 3 housekeeper 4 chandelier

7 9.04 **Listen to a story called *The Case of the Mysterious Fall*. Why is the fall mysterious?**

8 9.04 **Listen again. Mark the sentences T (true), F (false), or DS (doesn't say).**

1 Mr. Huntingdon was friendly and sociable. ☐
2 He only spoke to one person each week. ☐
3 He thought of a plan to try to cheat death. ☐
4 Mr. Huntingdon tried to call Mrs. Crabtree back to the house after she'd left. ☐
5 Mrs. Crabtree always started work at 8 a.m. ☐
6 The fortune teller's prediction came true. ☐

GRAMMAR

should(n't) have

9 Look at these sentences from the listening. Answer the questions. Then complete the rule.

1 Maybe [Mrs. Crabtree] should have asked why.
  a Did Mrs. Crabtree ask why?
  b Would it have been a good idea to?
2 He shouldn't have sent Mrs. Crabtree home.
  a Did Mr. Huntingdon send Mrs. Crabtree home?
  b Was it a good idea to?

RULE: To criticize actions in the past, we use ***should / shouldn't*** + [3]______ + the [4]______ form of the verb.

10 Write replies to the statements. Use *should have* or *shouldn't have* and suitable verbs. Then practice reading them out in pairs.

0 "I had five slices of pizza! Now I feel sick."
"You shouldn't have eaten so much pizza!"
1 "We've broken the TV. Quick! Put the ball away!"
2 "I bought these jeans yesterday, but now I don't have enough money to buy Mom a birthday present."
3 "I failed the test!"
4 "Joey didn't invite me to his party."
5 "You only paid $100 for those tickets? I paid $250!"

11 SPEAKING **Work in pairs. Write three sentences about famous people using *should have* or *shouldn't have*. Then read them out without saying the names. Your partner tries to guess who the people are.**

→ workbook page 82

THINK *values*

Thinking carefully before you act

12 SPEAKING **Work in pairs. Which do you think was Mr. Huntingdon's biggest mistake?**

A He should have thought about his plan more carefully.
B He should have told Mrs. Crabtree about the fortune teller's prediction.
C He shouldn't have gone to see the fortune teller.

13 SPEAKING **Look at the pictures. What mistake did each person make? What should they have done?**

1

3

2

4

READING

1 SPEAKING Look at the pictures. What do you see in them? Discuss your answers in pairs.

2 🔊 9.05 Read and listen to the article. Why do you think the photo of the dress went viral?

3 Read the article again. Find and match 1–6 with a–f.

1 ☐ started a family argument
2 ☐ sold the dress
3 ☐ became an internet sensation
4 ☐ set up a study
5 ☐ studied the photo
6 ☐ makes decisions about colors

a the brain
b researchers
c scientists
d the retailer
e the dress
f the photo of the dress

THE DRESS

It goes without saying that people love optical illusions – they've always been popular in books and pictures. Now, with social media, we've gone one step further and everyone is sharing these puzzling illusions. Here's one that was a smash hit with people all over the world.

Is it blue and black **or** white and gold? Which two colors would you go for? This is the story of how an ordinary dress became an internet sensation. You couldn't have missed it!

The mother of a bride sent her daughter a photo of a dress that she was planning to wear to the wedding and it started an argument between the daughter, her fiancé, and their friends. Some of them saw the dress as white and gold while others saw it as blue and black. How weird is that?

One friend posted the photo on the internet and the social media world went crazy. Within a week, the photo went viral and more than 10 million tweets mentioned the dress, using hashtags such as #thedress, #whiteandgold, and #blueandblack. The retailer confirmed that the actual color of the dress was blue and black, but the debate went on.

So why did people see the dress so differently? After reviewing the photo, scientists had some answers. The photo wasn't very clear, so when it was taken the dress could have been in shadow or in the light. And the lighting may have been natural daylight (which is blueish) or from an electric light (which is yellowish). That's important, because our brain depends on the light to decide what color things really are.

A group of researchers set up an online study to find out more. The study went well, as 8,000 people responded and the results were interesting. There was a big difference between "larks," who get up early and spend a lot of time in daylight, and "owls," who stay up late and are more used to artificial light. Larks usually saw the dress as white and gold and owls usually saw it as blue and black.

However, the researchers say that there might have been other reasons for the difference. The study showed that it wasn't important where people lived or what time of day they viewed the photo. But the size of their screen made a difference – people who saw the dress on a bigger screen were more likely to see it as white and gold. Also, women were a bit more likely than men to see it as white and gold. It seems there's still a lot to learn about how we see colors!

One thing is certain. As a result of all this attention on social media, sales of the dress went up dramatically. The retailer produced the dress in white and gold as well as blue and black and they must have made a lot of money!

GRAMMAR
Modals of deduction (past)

4 **Match 1–3 with a–c. Check your answers in the article on page 88. Then match sentences 1–3 with the rules.**

1 You can't have
2 The dress could have
3 The retailer must have

a made a lot of money!
b been in shadow or in the light.
c missed it!

RULE:
To say something was possibly the case in the past, we use *might* / *could* / *may* + *have* + past participle. ☐
To say something was definitely not the case in the past, we use *couldn't* / *can't* + *have* + past participle. ☐
To say something was definitely the case in the past, we use *must* + *have* + past participle. ☐

5 **Complete the conversation. Use suitable modals and the correct forms of the verbs in parentheses.**

"The Case of the Missing Cake"

Oliver What?! My cake! It's gone!
Matt Really?
Oliver Yes, it was here an hour ago and now it isn't. Who took it?
Matt What about Dad? I heard him saying how hungry he was. In fact, I'm sure it [1]__________ (be) Dad.
Oliver No, he [2]__________ (eat) it. It was chocolate. Dad doesn't like chocolate.
Matt That's true I suppose, Mom. [3]__________ (take) it, maybe?
Oliver No, it [4]__________ (be) Mom. She's been out all morning.
Matt The dog! He [5]__________ (jump) onto the table and eaten it. That dog's always doing things like that.
Oliver Are you crazy? The cake was in the fridge. The dog [6]__________ (get) into it.
Matt Are you sure it wasn't you? I mean, you [7]__________ (eat) it and forgotten.
Oliver I'm pretty sure it wasn't me. So if it wasn't me, Mom, Dad, or the dog, that leaves one person. It [8]__________ (be) you, Matt!
Matt What?! Me?
Oliver Yes, and that explains why you have chocolate all around your mouth!

→ workbook page 83

FUNCTIONS
Making deductions

6 **Read the text and complete the sentences with your opinions. Use *can't*, *must*, or *might*.**

In 1998, Russian scientists found a meteorite with a metal screw in it. The rock is at least 300 million years old. At that time, there weren't even any dinosaurs on the planet.

1 It ______ be fake.
2 There ______ have been intelligent life on Earth 300 million years ago.
3 I think someone ______ have made it as a joke.
4 It ______ be from another planet.
5 The scientists ______ have lied about it.

7 SPEAKING **Work in pairs. Discuss your ideas.**

VOCABULARY
Expressions with *go*

8 **Find expressions 1–8 in the text on page 88. Match them with the definitions.**

1 go for
2 go one step further
3 go viral
4 go well
5 go crazy
6 go up
7 go without saying
8 go on

a do something extra
b be satisfactory
c become very excited about something
d be obvious
e be shared by many people on the Internet
f continue
g choose
h increase

9 **Complete the sentences with the correct forms of the expressions in Exercise 8.**

1 The party's __________, I think. Everyone's having fun.
2 It __________ that your mom and I will support you in your decision!
3 The soccer fans __________ when their team won the game.
4 I __________ the red one. It's cool.
5 He posted the photo and within days it __________!
6 I drew a picture of my dream house. My brother __________ and built it.
7 The price of bread has continued to __________.
8 It was raining, but we still __________ playing. We didn't stop.

→ workbook page 84

Fiction

1 **Look at the picture. Make some predictions.**

- What do you think will happen to spoil this beautiful scene?
- What will happen to the woman in the red dress?
- Why will the flower seller get angry?

2 9.06 **Read and listen to the extract. Were your predictions correct?**

Wild Country by Margaret Johnson

Chapter 1 *The flower market mistake*

The woman in the red dress was holding some large yellow flowers to her face. Behind her, there were lots more flowers – big flowers, small flowers, flowers of every possible color. I was very pleased I'd got up early to see Nice's famous flower market. It was beautiful, and it helped me to forget that I wasn't going to have a nice day. Or a nice ten days. Grant Cooper! Grant Cooper! I couldn't believe I was going to work with that man for ten days. It was going to be horrible. But I wouldn't think about it until I had to. And here, in the market, I could almost forget. There was color all around me – not just the flowers, but also the people buying them in their summer clothes. Even the buildings behind the market were colorful – red and orange with blue windows. What a lovely picture it would make, if I only had my paints with me. But I did have a pencil somewhere. I could do a quick drawing. I still had a few minutes before I had to leave for the airport. I found the pencil in the bottom of my shoulder bag, together with an old letter. Soon my pencil was moving quickly over the back of the letter as I began to draw the woman in the red dress. She was smelling some red flowers now, and her hair was very blonde in the sunshine. As I drew what I saw, I quickly forgot about everything else. The woman buying the flowers obviously knew the flower seller. They were talking and laughing together, and I had lots of time to work on my picture.

I don't know how long I stood there. I only know that the next time I looked at my watch, it was nine o'clock. Nine o'clock! I only had thirty minutes to get to the airport. Oh no, I was going to be late. Again. But before I could put the pencil and paper back into my bag, I felt something soft against my legs. It was a small brown dog, and he was on his own. "Hello, boy," I said. "Are you lost?" The dog seemed to smile up at me, and I reached out to touch it. The dog smiled again, and then … it bit me! I screamed and jumped quickly back from the dog. Too quickly. There was a very loud crash behind me. "Mademoiselle!" shouted an angry voice. I turned round to see flowers all over the ground. "I'm sorry," I said. "That dog – it bit me!" "What dog?" asked the angry flower seller. "Well, that one," I said, but when I looked down, the dog had disappeared. "It was here a minute ago," I said, turning to look. Unfortunately, I turned so quickly that my shoulder bag flew through the air and crashed into some more flowers. "Mademoiselle!" shouted the flower seller again. "I'm sorry," I started to say, but then I noticed that things were about to get even worse. A river of dirty water from the flowers was moving very quickly towards the blonde woman's expensive white summer shoes. "Madame!" I shouted, but it was too late. "My shoes!" cried the blonde woman. "My flowers!" cried the flower seller. I held my hand up to show what the dog had done. "My finger!" I cried, but neither the flower seller nor the blonde woman was interested in my hurt finger.

3 9.06 **Read and listen to the extract again. Answer the questions.**

1 What did the flowers help the woman to forget?
2 What did she draw the picture on?
3 Why did she stop drawing?
4 Why did the woman jump backwards?
5 How did she knock over the second lot of flowers?
6 Why was the blonde woman upset?

4 SPEAKING **Work in pairs. Discuss these questions.**

1 Was the woman really bitten?
2 Will she find out more about the dog?
3 What will she find out?

WRITING
Explaining a mystery

1 INPUT **Read the article on the right. Who does the writer think is responsible for the crop circles?**

2 **Write the underlined expressions in the correct columns.**

I'm sure	I'm reasonably sure	I'm not sure

3 ANALYZE **The article has three paragraphs. What does the writer talk about in each one?**

4 PLAN **Read about a mystery. Then write three sentences about it. Use a different expression from Exercise 2 in each sentence.**

MISSING
HELICOPTER

An army helicopter with a pilot, co-pilot, and twelve soldiers on board has disappeared off the north coast of Scotland. The last contact with the helicopter was more than 12 hours ago, when the pilot radioed that everything was OK. No distress signal was received and despite a huge search over sea and land, no sign of the helicopter has been found. What happened to army helicopter 487?

5 PRODUCE **Write a blog entry (200 words) explaining what you think happened to the missing helicopter.**

Mysterious patterns
appear in local field overnight

1 This isn't the first time something like this happened and it probably won't be the last time either. For decades, crop circles have been fooling experts who are still asking, "What exactly causes these patterns?"

2 Some people say aliens might create this phenomenon. They suggest that aliens come to Earth at night and leave these patterns in our fields. These people are definitely wrong. Even if aliens from other planets existed, how could they land a huge spaceship without anyone noticing? It would be impossible, of course.

3 Humans must have made these crop circles, just as they must have made all the others, but I'm not certain how they did it. Obviously, it couldn't have been done by just one person; it must have been a group and more than likely, a really big one. Also, it's clear that the person or people behind the design must be extremely intelligent because these patterns are extraordinarily complex. It was most probably organized by a group of math students from a university. It's the kind of thing that students like to do as a joke. But whoever did it, they certainly got people talking.

10 MONEY

OBJECTIVES

FUNCTIONS: talking about future events; sympathizing

GRAMMAR: future continuous; future perfect

VOCABULARY: money and value; jobs and work; *by*

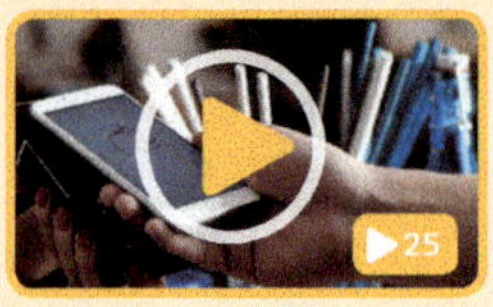

Get THINKING

Watch the video and think: do you think it would be possible to live without money?

READING

1 **Look at the photos and answer the questions.**

1 Which of the payment methods do you recognize? Where are they used?
2 Which of them do you or your family use?

2 **10.01 Read and listen to the article. Mark the sentences T (true) or F (false) according to the article.**

1 Paper money was invented because of the weight of coins. ☐
2 In Sweden, cash is disappearing. ☐
3 Supermarkets will never use invisible payments. ☐
4 It's good to have computers looking after money systems, because they are 100% reliable. ☐
5 Security measures aren't a concern when thinking about privacy issues. ☐
6 In the future, there might be payment systems we haven't thought of yet. ☐

Train to THINK

Exaggeration

Sometimes writers exaggerate to create dramatic effect. Of course, this doesn't mean that what they're saying is completely true.

3 **Look at these sentences from the article. Which words show that they're exaggerations?**

1 The answer is undeniably "no."
2 By far, that's the most important question.

4 **Read the sentences. Which *isn't* an exaggeration? Write the words that help you decide.**

1 There's no way that credit cards will exist in ten years.
2 I found this subject really interesting.
3 It's the best article that has ever been written.

5 **Rewrite these sentences so they contain an exaggeration.**

1 It was a really boring movie.
2 Justin Timberlake is a great singer.
3 Brian's good at math.

MONEY: PAST, PRESENT, AND FUTURE

Thousands of years ago, people started using metal coins as money to buy and sell things. But the coins were heavy, so paper money was invented. Different payment systems evolved through time and now we also use credit and debit cards. These cards often have to be put into a machine and then a PIN has to be entered – but that practice is disappearing with contactless cards and smartphone apps becoming more and more popular. So, cash has mostly been replaced by alternative payment methods. And things don't stop there; it's possible that some countries will soon be completely cashless. For example, it's predicted that no one in Sweden will be using cash at all by about 2025.

So, what is the future of money? Twenty years from now, will we still be using cash? The answer is undeniably "no." And it's highly likely that bank cards are on their way out as well. This is happening already: the use of smartphones, smartwatches, and electronic wristbands has allowed people, in many situations, to avoid using cash or cards. Some apps let us transfer money from phone to phone like a text message, which makes it a quick and easy way to repay a friend if you owe them money. Increasingly, people are making "invisible" payments for things like car rides – you choose a car, you take the ride, the money automatically comes out of your registered card. You can even include a tip for your driver this way! Perhaps we will soon be doing this in places like supermarkets, too – you'll get your goods, a reader will record the details of what you've bought as you leave and the amount will be taken automatically from your account. And if you need a refund, the money is put back in your account as easily as it was taken out.

Worry-free shopping. No machines or long check-out lines. No more heavy wallets or purses. This all sounds very positive, but there are possible disadvantages, too. Technological advancement, as we all know, brings many positives but also forces us to consider other matters. Will fraud, especially online, get easier? And as our money systems become more dependent on computers, how can we make sure that the computers don't fail? Security might get better as we increase our use of things like fingerprint and facial recognition, but will they be used to invade our privacy by gathering information about our movements? By far, that's the most important question.

Questions like these won't go away easily. We are in a state of change, and there are many different future possibilities. Perhaps unimagined payment methods will be developed. It will be interesting to see how things move forward, but one thing is for sure – in 20 years' time, we won't be buying, selling, or paying for things the same ways we do now.

SPEAKING

6 **Work in pairs. Discuss these questions.**

1 Do you think a cashless society would be a good idea? Why or why not?
2 Do you think there will still be coins and bills in 30 years' time? Why or why not?

GRAMMAR
Future continuous

1 Complete the sentences from the article on page 93. Then choose the correct words to complete the rule.

1 Twenty years from now, will __________ still __________ cash?

2 Perhaps we __________ soon __________ this in places like supermarkets, too.

3 In 20 years' time, we __________ buying, selling, and paying the same way that we do now.

> **RULE:** We use **the future continuous** to talk about things that will be in progress at [4]***a specified / an unspecified*** time in the future.

2 Complete the sentences with the correct forms of the verbs.

1 Tomorrow at ten o'clock, I __________ (sit) on a train.

2 Lucky you! This time next week, you __________ (enjoy) your vacation.

3 Susan is still in college, but a year from now, she __________ (work) in her dad's company.

4 What __________ I __________ (do) three years from now? I have no idea.

5 Talk to Sam now. Tonight he __________ (play) tennis, so you won't be able to reach him.

6 Tomorrow afternoon, we __________ (have) a coffee in a café next to the river.

3 Complete the text. Use the simple future or future continuous form of the verbs.

not travel | drink | wake up | put on
not work | pay | lie | have

I know where I'll be ten years from now. I [1]__________ 50 hours a week in a small office. I [2]__________ two hours every day to get to and from work. No, I [3]__________ on a beautiful Caribbean beach! I [4]__________ coconut water and reading a good book. Every day will be the same. I [5]__________ late and I [6]__________ a long, lazy breakfast. Every morning I [7]__________ my shorts and walk down to the beach to meet my friends. And how [8]__________ I __________ for all of this? That's an excellent question!

4 SPEAKING Work in pairs. Discuss what you will be doing at these times.

1 an hour from now
2 at eight o'clock tonight
3 this time next week
4 on January 1st

An hour from now, I'll be having lunch.

→ workbook page 90

VOCABULARY
Money and value

5 Match the words with the definitions.

a tip | $(X) off | a reward | a bargain
owe | a refund | be worth
not good value for money | valuable | on sale

1 money that you get for doing something helpful (for example, finding something that was lost)
2 money that's paid back to you (for example, if you return something to a store)
3 extra money to thank someone (for example, a waiter) for a service
4 to need to pay someone
5 available at a good price (usually for a short time)
6 money taken away from the original price
7 something you get at a really good price
8 not worth its price
9 having a very high value
10 to have a value of

6 Complete the sentences with the words from Exercise 5.

0 I'm not buying the shoes in this store. There's another one nearby where they're *on sale* .
1 I ______ Kylie $20. I mustn't forget to repay her.
2 Mr. Brown offered a big ______ for any information that would help him to find his cat.
3 The taxi driver was very helpful, so we gave him a good ______ .
4 Have a look at this old coin. Do you think it's ______ much?
5 I bought this expensive laptop last week. Today I saw it in the store for $100 ______ .
6 The tablet didn't work, so I took it back to the store and they gave me a ______ .
7 I paid $50 for this toy and it broke after a week. It really was ______ .
8 I waited until after the holiday and got the bike for half price. It was a real ______ .
9 This vase is 3,000 years old and very ______ .

7 SPEAKING **Work in pairs. Discuss the questions.**

1 What's the most valuable thing that teenagers usually own?
2 What are some good ways to get a bargain?
3 In what situations might you give someone a reward or a tip? Have you ever received one?
4 Have you ever had to ask for a refund? What for?

→ workbook page 92

LISTENING

8 **Look at the questionnaire and try to guess the answers. Then compare with a partner.**

9 10.02 **Listen to an extract from the quiz show *Moneyspinners*. Check your answers.**

WordWise: Phrases with *by*

10 **What do the phrases in bold refer to? Match 1–4 with a–d.**

1 Cash has mostly been replaced **by alternative payment methods.** ☐
2 She won $1,000 **by answering** questions about money. ☐
3 You can get money from the cash machine **by the entrance** to the supermarket. ☐
4 No one in Sweden will be using cash at all **by 2025.** ☐

a a location
b a time in the future
c a way to do something
d the person / people / thing(s) that do something

11 **Complete the sentences with the phrases.**

by the bus station | by the end of class
by the French teacher | by washing

1 Please finish Exercise 2 ________________ .
2 I was made to stay after class ________________ .
3 Meet me tomorrow ________________ downtown.
4 I made some money ________________ people's cars.

→ workbook page 92

PRONUNCIATION
Short and long vowel sounds: /ɪ/ – /iː/ and /ɑ/ – /oʊ/ Go to page 121.

ODD FACTS ABOUT MONEY

1 **Some coins in … have holes in the middle.**
A Britain
B Iceland
C Japan
D South Africa

2 **More people take money out of automatic teller machines (ATMs) on … than any other day.**
A Mondays
B Thursdays
C Fridays
D Saturdays

3 **Of all the money in the world, only … is actual cash (coins and bills).**
A 8%
B 12%
C 20%
D 50%

4 **The first country to make plastic bills was …**
A Sweden.
B Germany.
C the US.
D Australia.

5 **The world's first known coin is called the …**
A Egyptian Lira.
B Lydian Lion.
C Ying Yuan.
D Saxon Shilling.

READING

1 **Look at the people in the photographs. If Margaret Phelps earns $95,000 a year, how much do you think the other two get?**

2 **Read the article and posts quickly. Choose a suitable title.**

A Inequality isn't only about money
B A new kind of inequality
C Equality is impossible
D Continued inequality

3 10.05 **Read and listen to the article and posts. Which writer thinks ...**

1 it's not always ability that determines who gets rich and who doesn't?
2 people can get good jobs because of who they know?
3 high salaries are OK because earners contribute to society?
4 differences in salaries are just part of life?
5 healthcare managers shouldn't earn more than medical professionals?
6 it's possible to earn a lot of money before you're very old?

MONEY**MATTERS**

HOME BLOG LOGIN

____

It's said that the easiest way to be really rich is to be born into a really rich family. That aside, undoubtedly the best way to become truly wealthy is to get a good idea for a product, make it, and sell it, then sit back and watch the money come in. Throughout history, many people have become incredibly wealthy that way.

There's nothing new in this – for centuries people have had ideas, made things, and become very rich. But questions are increasingly being asked about the way we're going. How fair is it for one person to have a personal fortune of billions of dollars? Is it right for big company bosses to be paid huge salaries and often to receive large bonuses on top of that? In just one year, the head of a real estate company in the US received $29 million in bonuses. Is that acceptable? In 1965, bosses in the US's biggest companies earned on average about 20 times an ordinary employee's salary – in 1978 it was 30 times, but by 2020, this had increased to 70 times. However, some CEOs make more than 400 times what their employees make.

We'd like to hear your comments on this subject. 5 20 9

A I finished high school with a guy I know and we went to work in a finance company. His father's one of the directors, so now he has a very well-paid job, earning five times as much as me. By the time he's 30, he'll have earned millions – and he does everything he can to avoid paying taxes. It's sickening.

GBarker95

B I'm not sure what the problem is. It's just how the world is. Like the article says, there's nothing new here. Some people get lucky, some don't. Look at writers – lots of people get an idea and write a book or books – and sometimes thousands of people buy the book and the writer gets rich. They're not even always the best writers. That's just how it is.

Thatcherman

C One time, I heard a politician say, "It's fine for people to be extremely rich – as long as they pay their taxes." I agree. A top boss, after ten years of work or so, will have given millions of dollars back in taxes to help the country. And that benefits everyone, right?

Arguer123

D My mom's a doctor and she'll be working until she's 60 – 35 years of work – and when she stops, she won't have made a tenth of what some of these people make in a year. And there are people who manage the hospitals she works in who earn five times what she does. Who contributes more to healthcare – a doctor or someone who works in management? It's disgraceful.

Aliboy

GRAMMAR
Future perfect

4 Complete the sentences from the comments on page 96. Then read the rule and complete it with the words in the list.

1 A top boss, after ten years of work or so, ______________ millions of dollars back in taxes.

2 When she stops, she ______________ a tenth of what some of these people make in a year.

have | past participle | *will*

RULE: We use the future perfect to talk about actions that will finish at some time between now and a specified time in the future.

now — $1 million — $2 million — $3 million — end of the year

By the end of the year, he'll have made more than $3 million.

- We form it with [3]______ + [4]______ + [5]______ .
- We often use it with *by* + a point in time or *by the time* + a time clause.
  By 2050, …
  By the time I'm 50, …

5 Complete the sentences with the future perfect form of the verbs.

1 The government ______________ (build) lots of new houses here by 2030.

2 By the time I'm 35, I ______________ (work) in IT for over ten years.

3 If I work really hard, I ______________ (do) my homework by the time the game starts on TV.

4 The test is from 9 to 12 tomorrow morning. So at ten o'clock, I ______________ (not finish) it.

5 By that time, I ______________ (buy) my first house.

6 I hope that three years from now, I ______________ (visit) one or two other countries.

6 SPEAKING Work in pairs. Look at the questions and make notes. Then compare your ideas.

1 Which tasks will / won't you have finished by 6 p.m. tomorrow?

2 What will / won't you have done by the end of the year?

3 Which goals will you have achieved six years from now?

→ workbook page 90

VOCABULARY
Jobs and work

7 Match the words with the definitions.

education | employee | employer | finance | healthcare | law | management | public service | qualifications | salary

1 abilities or experience needed for a particular job
2 jobs paid for by the government
3 people who make the big decisions in a company
4 teaching and learning
5 a person or organization that people work for
6 an area of work related to managing money
7 the money a person is paid for doing a job
8 an area of work related to the legal system
9 an area of work related to medicine
10 someone who's paid to work for someone else

8 Complete the sentences with words from Exercise 7.

1 Her dad works in ______ . He's a nurse.
2 Margaret Bourne is the director of ______ for a big company. She decides on all the investments.
3 Joanna was a police officer and now she's a teacher. She's been in ______ all her professional life.
4 Larry is a teacher. He works in ______ .
5 The company suffered years of bad ______ .
6 This tech company is the biggest ______ in the Seattle area.
7 A degree and some experience in IT are necessary ______ for this job.
8 James works in the ______ . He's a judge.
9 Allan got a new job with a higher ______ .
10 She's been an ______ of this company for 25 years.

9 SPEAKING Work in pairs. Discuss these questions.

1 Which of the areas of work in Exercise 7 would you be most / least interested in? Why?
2 Would you rather be an employer or an employee? Why?

→ workbook page 92

WRITING
My life in the future

10 Write about your life 30 years from now (150–200 words). Think about the things that you:

- will be doing.
- won't have done.
- will have done.
- will still want to do.

DEVELOPING SPEAKING

1 10.06 **Look at the photo. Where are the three people? What do you think they're talking about? Read and listen to check.**

Josh: That was a delicious cookie. I wish I could buy another one – but I'm really strapped for cash, <u>same as usual</u>.

Tanya: <u>Don't look at me</u>. Sorry, but I only have enough for my ice cream. Last week, I had to fix my bike. So <u>I'm broke</u>.

Josh: What a shame. Never mind, though, you'll get some spending money soon, won't you?

Tanya: I hate not having money to do the things I want. My grandparents have spent their whole lives like that. Not me. I'm determined to be seriously rich when I'm older.

Josh: Your grandparents seem really happy to me. Maybe they never worried about material things.

Tanya: So I'm wrong to want to be rich?

Josh: No, I'm saying not everyone wants to be, <u>that's all</u>. You can be happy without a lot of money.

Tanya: I'm just ambitious. <u>It's not my fault</u>.

Mark: Hi, guys! All right?

Josh: Not bad, Mark. We're talking about money – or rather, not having it. We're both broke, basically.

Mark: That's too bad. But good news. I've had some luck. I sold my tablet online for $50. The food and drinks <u>are on me</u>! What do you guys want?

Tanya: An ice cream please – and another cookie for Josh?

Josh: No, I'm fine thanks. You should keep your money.

Mark: No, money's for spending as far as I'm concerned. OK, then: one ice cream for Tanya and two for me!

2 10.06 **Listen and read the dialogue again. Answer the questions.**

1 Why doesn't Tanya have any money?
2 Why doesn't she want to be like her grandparents?
3 How much did Mark sell his tablet for?
4 Who is going to buy food and drinks?

3 SPEAKING **Discuss the statements in pairs. Which do you agree with (if any)?**

1 I'm determined to be seriously rich when I'm older.
2 You can be happy without a lot of money.
3 Money's for spending as far as I'm concerned.

Phrases for fluency

4 **Find the underlined expressions in the dialogue. How do you say them in your language? Use the expressions to complete the dialogues.**

1 A I don't have enough money for lunch.
B Well, ____________________ ! I can't pay because ____________________ – again!
C It's OK. I'll pay for the food. Lunch and drinks ____________________ !

2 A Hi, Jack. How are you?
B Oh, ____________________ , really. Nothing changes a lot, does it?

3 A Wow, this room is really messy!
B Hey! ____________________ ! Julie made the mess, not me.
C OK, calm down. I didn't say it was you. I just said it was messy, ____________________ .

FUNCTIONS
Sympathizing

KEY LANGUAGE
I'm really sorry (to hear that).
That's too bad.
How awful.
What a shame.
Never mind.

5 **Look back at the dialogue. Complete the extracts with some phrases from the Key Language box.**

Tanya So, I'm broke.
Josh [1] ____________________ ! [2] ____________________ though, you'll get some spending money soon.
Josh We're both broke, basically.
Mark [3] ____________________ !

6 SPEAKING **Work in pairs. Write two-line conversations like the one in Exercise 5 about each of these situations. Then act them out.**

You tell your friend that …
- your exam results are very bad.
- you lost some money.
- you broke your smartphone.

LIFE COMPETENCIES

Being determined is a positive quality to have and it's good to want to achieve things in life.

1 ▶ 27 **Watch the vlog. Match these people with the roles they play in Serena's dream of learning the guitar?**

1 her dad	a her mentor
2 her music teacher	b her motivation
3 her friends	c her inspiration

2 ▶ 27 **Watch the vlog again and answer the questions.**

1 How is she going to find the time to learn the guitar?
2 How did her dad inspire her?
3 What advice did her teacher give her?
4 What is she going to do with her friends?

3 **Read the text. What is Harry's goal?**

Last year, my aunt got sick with cancer. She has spent a year getting treatment and she's recovering now, but I felt that I wanted to do something for her and other people who are sick. So, in two months' time, I am doing a half marathon to raise money for a cancer charity. I'm not very good at running and during the first month of training, I hurt my ankle. My training also started in January when it was cold and often dark. It's been tough sometimes, but I'm so grateful to my mom, who encouraged me and ran with me on the cold mornings. So far I've raised $400 and I'm hoping to raise $500. My aunt is really proud of me, so I'm determined to finish for her.
Harry

4 **Answer the questions about the text.**

1 What difficulties has Harry had to overcome to try to reach his goal?
2 What kind of special motivation does he have for being determined?
3 How much money has he raised?
4 How are other people helping him to achieve his goal?

Me and my world

5 **Think of a time you were determined to do something and make notes.**

- What did you want to do?
- Why did you want to do it?
- Were you successful?
- How did the experience make you feel?

6 **Talk to your friend about the experience.**

TIPS FOR BEING DETERMINED

- Try not to get discouraged – don't give up if things don't work out for you at first.
- Being determined isn't the only thing that counts. Remember to think about how your actions might affect the people around you.
- It's OK to accept help even when you were determined to complete a task alone.

TOWARDS B2 First for Schools

LISTENING
Sentence completion

→ workbook page 89

1 10.07 **You will hear Conner talking about the Royal Mint, where coins are made. For questions 1–10, complete the sentences with a word or short phrase.**

Someone who collects [1]____________________ is known as a numismatist.
The Royal Mint is the [2]____________________ mint in the world.
The Mint doesn't make [3]____________________ ; that's the responsibility of the Bank of England.
When the Mint started, [4]____________________ ruled England.
Work at the Royal Mint never [5]____________________ .
In one [6]____________________ , the Mint can produce 90 million coins.
The Mint produces coins for [7]____________________ different nations as well as the UK.
A metal disc with nothing printed on it is called a [8]____________________ .
In 2012, the Mint made coins to commemorate the [9]____________________ and the Queen's Diamond Jubilee.
Because of security concerns, you can't [10]____________________ the Royal Mint.

WRITING
Essay

→ workbook page 97

2 **In your English class, you have been talking about money. Now your English teacher has asked you to write an essay for homework.**

Write your essay using all the notes and giving reasons for your point of view. Give your opinion (for or against) in the last paragraph.

Is it more important to enjoy your job or to earn a lot of money?

Notes – write about:

1 material possessions
2 happiness and job satisfaction
3 ____________________ (your own idea).

Write your essay in 140–190 words.

TEST YOURSELF UNITS 9 & 10

VOCABULARY

1 Complete the sentences with the words / phrases in the list. There are four extra words / phrases.

unexplained | went on | bargain | mysterious | worth | employer | on sale
employee | alien | refund | go very well | owe | going for | salary

1 He's worked for that company for 25 years now. He's their oldest ____________________ .
2 Nobody knows what happened to him. The mystery of his disappearance is still ____________________ .
3 The rain was terrible, but the race ____________________ despite it.
4 Michael lent me some money last month. I still ____________________ him 75 cents.
5 I bought this camera for half price. It was a real ____________________ !
6 You paid too much for it. It isn't ____________________ that much money.
7 I'm afraid the exam didn't ____________________ . I'm sure I failed it.
8 He's been training all year. He's ____________________ a gold medal.
9 You know those sneakers you like? They're ____________________ at the moment! You should buy them.
10 It's broken. I think you should take it back and ask for a ____________________ .

/10

GRAMMAR

2 Complete the sentences with the verbs in the list. There are two extra verbs.

might | should have | won't be working | must have | might have
will be living | will have written | couldn't have

1 She hurt her head when she fell off her scooter. She ____________________ worn a helmet.
2 She's a really good runner. If she'd entered the race, she ____________________ won it.
3 By the time I'm 25, I ____________________ on a Greek island!
4 In ten years' time, I ____________________ for anybody. I'll have my own company.
5 He got there too late. He ____________________ prevented the accident.
6 By the time I'm 30, I ____________________ my first novel.

3 Find and correct the mistake in each sentence.

1 He shouldn't has left the window open. That's how the burglar got in.
2 She might like the movie if she had come.
3 In ten years' time, I hope I will have working in London.
4 Where will you living in 20 years' time?
5 He must be finished his homework by now.
6 In five years' time, I will have climb Mount Everest.

/12

FUNCTIONAL LANGUAGE

4 Choose the correct words.

1 A No way! This piece of rock *can't* / *mustn't* be from another planet.
B I don't agree with you. I think it *can* / *might* be.
2 A I'm *many* / *really* sorry I can't come to the soccer game with you.
B Never *mind* / *know*. You can come with me next week.
3 A Hi, guys. What would you like to eat? The food's *on* / *with* me!
B Great! Same as *normal* / *usual*, please!
4 A It goes without *seeing* / *saying* that Peter can't come on Saturday. He crashed his scooter.
B How *shameful* / *awful*!

/8

MY SCORE /30

22–30 | 10–21 | 0–9

11 EMERGENCY!

OBJECTIVES

FUNCTIONS:
expressing purpose; emphasizing

GRAMMAR:
verbs followed by gerund or infinitive; *to / in order to / so as to; so* and *such*

VOCABULARY:
danger and safety; adjectives with negative prefixes

Get THINKING

Watch the video and think: have you ever been in a dangerous situation? What happened?

A

B

C

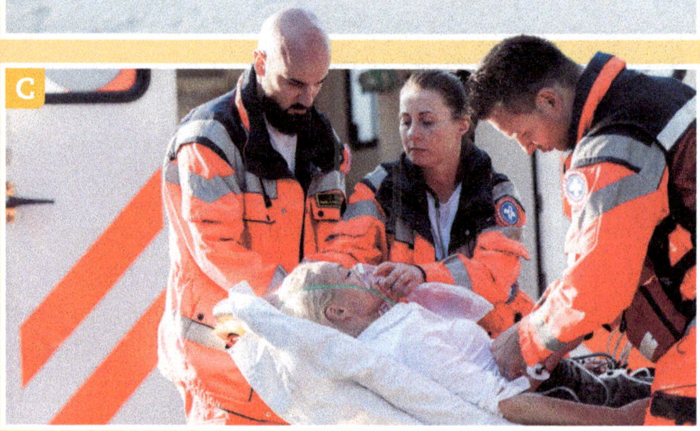

READING

1 **Look at the photos. What is the same about all of them? What is different in each one?**

2 **Read the sentences. Which photo(s) might each one refer to?**

1 It took the rescuers a long time to bring the victim down. ☐
2 The victim was given first aid before going to the hospital. ☐
3 The helicopter emergency services managed to pull the victim out of the water. ☐
4 After the rescue operation, the victim was taken to the hospital for treatment. ☐

3 **Make a list of people and things that can help in an emergency. Compare your ideas with others in the class.**

Things	People
ambulance	*police officer*

4 **Look at the photos on the next page and the title of the news report. What do you think it's about? Read the report quickly and check your ideas.**

5 11.01 **Read and listen to the report. Mark the sentences T (true) or F (false).**

1 The boys had just finished playing a soccer game. ☐
2 There is no complete map of the caves. ☐
3 You can get a guided tour of the beginning of the cave all year round. ☐
4 It was two days before the police knew where the boys were. ☐
5 The rescue quickly turned into an international mission. ☐
6 The boys had been missing for two weeks before contact was made with them. ☐
7 The divers knew they had to get the boys out quickly. ☐
8 The boys had to dive through the tunnels to get to safety. ☐

Miracle UNDERGROUND

It was June 23rd, 2018. Twelve members of the Wild Boars soccer team and their coach stood in front of the entrance to the Tham Luang cave in northern Thailand. The boys, aged between 11 and 16, had finished training for the day and they decided to explore the cave. They left their bikes outside and took their flashlights and some snacks inside with them. It would be more than two weeks before the group saw daylight again.

The Tham Luang cave stretches 10 km into the mountain with a network of chambers, narrow passages, and tunnels. Parts of the cave have been explored, but much of it hasn't. Inside, there is no phone signal, so contact with the outside world is impossible. The first kilometer is open to the public, but only until June. In the rainy season from July to November, it becomes extremely dangerous because the whole system quickly fills with water. And in June of 2018, the rain came early.

When the boys failed to come home that evening, their parents contacted the police. Finding the bikes outside the cave, the police soon realized where they were, but they also knew that rainwater had flooded the caves. The boys and their coach were trapped somewhere inside and were in great danger.

At 4 a.m. the next morning, Thai divers tried to start searching the cave, but it was soon clear that they did not have the equipment or experience they needed. News of the emergency soon spread. Within days, experts from countries all over the world had arrived at the cave hoping to help rescue the group.

For days, an international team of divers searched deep into the caves, but found no sign of the group. Then, at last, on the tenth day, two British divers arrived in a new chamber where they saw 13 figures sitting on a shelf of rock above the water. The boys and their coach were very thin and weak, but they were alive. The celebrations, though, were short. The divers knew the boys weren't out of danger yet and that the rescue would be extremely difficult. They had 13 young people with no diving experience to bring to safety through 4 km of dark, narrow passages. Furthermore, heavy rain was predicted and water levels would soon be rising. If they weren't brought out soon, it would be impossible to save them.

A team of experts worked night and day to plan the rescue. Each boy, dressed in a wetsuit and with a supply of oxygen, was taken underwater by a diver through the flooded chambers. The divers were guided by ropes to avoid losing their way and they kept checking the air bubbles to make sure the boys were breathing. In other parts of the cave, the boys lay on plastic stretchers, which were pushed with great difficulty through the narrow spaces.

It took three days to get everyone to safety and the last person was brought out just as the water levels in the cave started to rise quickly. It was a miracle – all 13 members of the Wild Boars had survived.

Train to THINK

Understanding cause and effect

There is a cause-and-effect relationship between two ideas only if we can show that one thing leads to another.

6 Match the causes (1–5) with the effects (a–e). Then check your answers in the article.

1 The boys didn't come home. ☐
2 The police found the boys' bikes. ☐
3 It had rained a lot overnight. ☐
4 News of the emergency spread. ☐
5 The boys had been missing for ten days. ☐

a Experts from all over the world arrived to help.
b Most people thought they were dead.
c The caves were flooded.
d They knew the boys were in the cave.
e The parents contacted the police.

7 Complete 1–3 with a cause or an effect.

1 The flooding became worse, so the divers …
2 … , so we decided to call the emergency services.
3 … Therefore, the victim was taken to the hospital.

SPEAKING

8 Work in pairs. Discuss these questions.

1 Do you think the divers were heroes? Why or why not?
2 Do you know any stories of ordinary people being heroes?

GRAMMAR
Verbs followed by gerund or infinitive

1 **Complete the sentences from the news report on page 103. What do the verbs have in common?**

1 They decided ______ the caves.
2 The boys failed ______ home.
3 They hoped ______ rescue the group.

2 **Now complete these sentences from the report. What do these verbs have in common? Then complete the rule. Label the columns with *to + infinitive* or *gerund*.**

1 The boys, aged between 11 and 16, had finished ______ for the day.
2 The divers were guided by ropes to avoid ______ their way.
3 Divers kept ______ the air bubbles.

RULE:

Followed by [4] ______	Followed by [5] ______
avoid, enjoy, feel like, finish, imagine, keep, (don't) mind, miss, practice, (can't) stand, suggest	afford, choose, decide, expect, fail, hope, learn, offer, promise, want

3 **Complete the sentences. Use a verb from A followed by a verb from B in each sentence.**

A avoid | ~~choose~~ | decide | feel like | finish | hope
B buy | go | see | speak | ~~stay~~ | watch

0 I can't believe you *chose to stay* at home last night rather than come to the movies with us.
1 After a lot of thought, I ______ a new bike.
2 Bye! I ______ you again soon.
3 I'm so tired. I just ______ to bed.
4 I really don't like him, so I ______ to him.
5 I'll help you. I'll just ______ this video first.

→ workbook page 100

PRONUNCIATION
Strong and weak forms: /tuː/ and /tə/
Go to page 121.

VOCABULARY
Danger and safety

4 **Replace the underlined phrases with the words and phrases in the list.**

rescued | dangerous | in danger | to safety | survived | recover | save his life | out of danger

1 He was in a terrible accident, but he <u>didn't die</u>.
2 Don't go into that room! There might be something <u>that could hurt you</u> in there.
3 She went to the hospital to <u>get better</u>.
4 The firefighter <u>took</u> the baby <u>away from a dangerous situation</u>.
5 The doctors managed to <u>prevent him from dying</u>.
6 People who lived near the volcano moved away so they were <u>not going to be harmed</u>.
7 People who drive really fast sometimes put their lives <u>in a situation where they are likely to be harmed</u>.
8 The helicopter took him <u>to a place where he wasn't going to be harmed</u>.

5 **Choose the correct words.**

1 Thank you so much – you *rescued / saved* my life!
2 We can go in here. It isn't *safe / dangerous* at all.
3 We were lucky to *survive / save* the accident.
4 The boat sank, but all the passengers were *recovered / rescued* by another boat.
5 Fortunately, he *recovered / saved* from his injuries.
6 No one died. All the passengers *rescued / survived*.
7 She was badly hurt in the accident, but fortunately she's *in / out of* danger now.
8 The helicopter flew the survivors *in danger / to safety*.

6 SPEAKING **Work in pairs or small groups. Discuss these questions.**

1 In which sports and activities are people in danger? Do you do them? Would you like to? Why or why not?
2 Do you know of someone who has been in a bad accident and survived? How did he/she survive?
3 Do you know anyone who's saved another person's life? Who was it? What happened?

→ workbook page 102

LISTENING

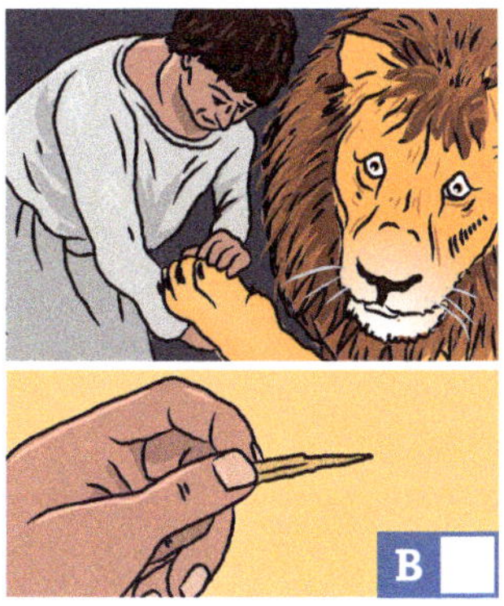

7 In which picture can you see these things?

arena | emperor | gate | master
paw | slave | thorn

8 🔊 11.04 **You're going to hear a story called *Androcles and the Lion*. Put the pictures in the order you think tells the story. Then listen and check.**

9 🔊 11.04 **Listen again. Answer the questions.**

1 Why didn't Androcles run from the lion in the forest?
2 Why did his master want to execute Androcles?
3 Why didn't the lion attack Androcles?
4 What did the emperor do and why?
5 What does the host think the moral is?

10 SPEAKING **Work in pairs or small groups. What do you think the moral of the story is? Do you know any other stories with morals?**

11 SPEAKING **Mark these statements 1–5 (1 = I strongly agree; 5 = I strongly disagree). Then discuss your answers in small groups.**

1 Helping someone else makes me feel good. ☐
2 I only help someone when they ask me to. ☐
3 You can always help another person. ☐
4 I only help people when I think they can also help me. ☐
5 I try to do something myself before I ask for help. ☐

GRAMMAR

to / in order to / so as to

12 Look at the sentences from the listening. Then complete the rule.

1 Androcles managed to escape and went to the forest to hide.
2 Androcles took it in his hand so as to see what the problem was.
3 The lion was kept in a cage for days without food in order to make him as hungry as possible.

> **RULE:** We can use ***to*** + infinitive to talk about purpose. In more formal language or in writing, we can also use [4]______ or [5]______ + infinitive.

13 Think about the stories in the unit so far. Match 1–4 with a–d. Then rewrite each pair as one sentence using the words in parentheses.

0 Why did Androcles pull the thorn from the lion's paw? *e*
Androcles pulled the thorn from the lion's paw to help the lion.
1 Why did the divers use ropes? ☐
2 Why did the international divers go to Thailand? ☐
3 Why did the boys need oxygen? ☐
4 Why was the lion put into the arena? ☐

a help the boys breathe underwater. (to)
b kill Androcles. (in order to)
c avoid losing their way. (so as to)
d help save the boys. (in order to)
e ~~help the lion~~. (to)

→ workbook page 100

FUNCTIONS

Expressing purpose

14 Match 1–5 with a–e.

1 Why did she send you a card? ☐
2 Why did you get up early yesterday? ☐
3 Why did you go into town? ☐
4 Why did he save his money for so long? ☐
5 Why did they move? ☐

a to watch the sun come up
b in order to get a new guitar
c so as to have more room
d to get a present for my mom
e to say thank you

15 SPEAKING **Work in pairs. Think of three *Why do / did you …?* questions to ask your partner. Ask and answer each other's questions.**

READING

1 In the US, you dial 911 for the emergency services. What number do you call in your country? Does it depend on the type of emergency?

2 11.05 Read and listen to the article. Which of the "emergency" calls do pictures A–C show?

EMERGENCY? *What emergency?*

An emergency service should be exactly that: a service that you call in an emergency. You might need to call an ambulance if you're in a car accident or the police if you see a crime happening. But some people call emergency services for such unimportant reasons that it's hard to believe these calls are real. Then again, there are some strange people out there, so maybe it isn't really so surprising that the emergency services get some unusual calls.

1 One soccer fan was so angry that his team, Manchester United, had lost an extremely important game that he called emergency services after the match and demanded to speak to the team's manager, Sir Alex Ferguson.

2 There was also a man who called the police after his son refused to get off his video game console late at night. He said they'd had such a bad argument that he wanted them to come and put the boy to bed.

3 One woman couldn't find her glasses and thought the emergency services might help. She complained that she was trying to peel potatoes, but her eyesight was so bad that she couldn't see what she was doing.

4 Once, a man dialed 911 when he found that his snowman had gone missing. He had left his house for five hours to find that it was gone when he returned. He said he was really angry and wanted the police to check security camera footage of the area.

5 The emergency services received a call from a woman to tell them that she had such a bad memory that she couldn't remember the password for her computer. She was so disappointed when they explained that they couldn't help her.

6 When one man's friend threw his shoes onto a supermarket roof as a joke, he called 911 and asked if the fire engine could come and help him get them down. He even offered to climb up to the roof himself if they could just bring a ladder.

7 One woman called up to complain that her husband was such a lazy man because he wouldn't bring her her dinner while she sat and watched TV.

8 Finally, one time a woman was so upset about a squirrel in her yard that didn't have any nuts that she called to say she wanted emergency services to find someone to bring it some food. She was worried it would starve.

These calls are amusing to read about, but they can have very serious consequences. "It's such a waste of time! Every call takes about a minute," said one man who works in the call center for the emergency services. "Maybe that doesn't sound a very long time, but in that one minute, other people are calling who really have an emergency. And for them, a minute might be extremely important."

So let's get serious: please THINK before you call emergency services. And, of course, remember that you should never call them with information that's untrue – it's irresponsible and it's also illegal.

3 **Read the first and last paragraphs again. Answer the questions.**

1 What examples are given of real emergencies?
2 Why should you never call emergency services with untrue information?

4 SPEAKING **Work in small groups. Which of the calls do you think was the craziest?**

GRAMMAR
so and *such*

5 Complete the sentences from the article on page 106. Then complete the rule.

1 She was ______ disappointed when they explained that they couldn't help her.
2 One woman called up to complain that her husband was ______ a lazy man.

> **RULE:** We can use ***so*** or ***such*** to emphasize adjectives, adverbs, nouns, and noun phrases:
> [1]______ + adjective / adverb
> [2]______ (+ ***a*** / ***an***) (+ adjective) + noun

6 Now complete these sentences from the article and complete the rule.

1 She had ______ that she couldn't remember the password for her computer.
2 Her eyesight was ______ that she couldn't see what she was doing.
3 They'd had ______ that he wanted the police to come and put the boy to bed.
4 One man was ______ that his team, Manchester United, had lost an extremely important game that he called emergency services.

> **RULE:** We also use ***so*** or ***such*** to show how one thing is a result of another. The clause with ***so*** or ***such*** is followed by ______ + a result clause.

7 Join the pairs of sentences. Use *so* / *such* ... *that*.

0 We were very late. We had to take a taxi.
We were so late that we had to take a taxi.
1 It was a very bad accident. Two people had to go to the hospital.
2 It was very windy. It was dangerous to walk there.
3 The music was very loud. I couldn't fall asleep.
4 The road was very icy. It was dangerous to drive on it.
5 They were careless people. They always forgot to lock the door to their house.

→ workbook page 101

VOCABULARY
Adjectives with negative prefixes

8 Replace the underlined words with one word.

0 The divers were not concerned about their own safety.
unconcerned
1 It was not possible to get the boys out together.
2 The Manchester United fan was not happy because his team had lost.
3 It's not surprising that the emergency services get so many crazy calls.
4 Some people call 911 for not important reasons.
5 These not necessary calls take up a lot of time.
6 You should never call with information that's not true – it's not responsible and it's also not legal.

9 Which negative prefixes do these adjectives take? Write them in the correct columns.

afraid | comfortable | concerned
expensive | formal | healthy | helpful
legal | logical | patient | polite
possible | regular | responsible | ~~surprising~~

un–	im–	in–	ir–	il–
unsurprising				

10 Complete the questions. Use adjectives from Exercise 9 with negative prefixes.

0 Do you think it's very *impolite* to talk with food in your mouth?
1 Do you think it's ______ to eat fried food?
2 Do you worry about exams, or are you ______ ?
3 Do you sometimes get a little ______ when you have to wait for things?
4 Do your parents think you're too ______ to be at home alone all weekend?
5 Do you think that ______ clothes are always bad quality?

11 SPEAKING Work in pairs. Discuss the questions in Exercise 10.

→ workbook page 102

THINK
The Great Escape

Culture

1 Look at the photos. What type of survival stories do they suggest?

2 11.06 Read and listen to the article. Check your answers.

The Great ESCAPE

After many tragedies, there are always stories of people who have shown an amazing ability to survive. Here are two stories that remind us that miracles can happen.

On August 5th, 2010, the San José copper and gold mine in the Atacama Desert in Chile collapsed and 33 miners were trapped underground. The mine had a poor safety record and there were fears that the missing men wouldn't come out alive. A rescue team immediately began drilling into the ground where it was thought the men might be. On Day 17, when the drill was brought out of the ground, there was a note taped to it. In bright red letters it read: "We are alive and well in the shelter, all 33 of us." It was the news the whole country had been waiting for and the Chilean government promised to bring them out alive. For the next seven weeks, rescue teams from all over the world worked together to drill a hole big enough to bring out the men, who were waiting 700 meters below the ground. It was a long, difficult, and dangerous job, but on October 13th, more than a billion people around the world watched live on TV as the first of the miners was finally brought above ground. Twenty-four hours later, the last miner, number 33, was reunited with his family and friends.

A

B

In June of 2013, a rescue diver was swimming through the wreck of the tugboat *Jascon-4* when he got an enormous shock: a hand reached out and grabbed his leg. The ship had sunk two and a half days earlier and was now lying 30 meters below the surface of the water. The diver, who was part of a team looking for the bodies of the 13 crew members, hadn't expected to find anyone alive. But one man had managed to survive. Twenty-nine-year-old Harrison Okene from Nigeria was the ship's cook. When the ship got into trouble in rough seas and started turning over, Okene found an air pocket and put his head in it. As the ship sank towards the ocean floor, he expected the pocket to fill with water, but it didn't. Despite the freezing water and having nothing to eat or drink, Okene had enough air to breathe. There was nothing he could do except wait. Sixty hours after the ship went down, Okene heard knocking and knew that rescue teams had entered the ship. He still wasn't safe and a complicated plan was needed to bring him slowly to the surface. Unfortunately, none of the other crew members survived. But for one man, the tragedy had ended with a miracle.

3 **Read the article again. What do these numbers refer to?**

0 7 *The number of weeks the miners were trapped underground.*

1 13 2 17 3 29
4 30 5 33 6 60

4 SPEAKING **Work in pairs. Discuss these questions.**

1 What do you think these people did while they were waiting to be rescued?
2 These people had accidents at work. Do you think people should be rescued when they are doing dangerous things for pleasure, like climbing mountains? Why or why not?

5 VOCABULARY **There are seven highlighted words or phrases in the article. Match the words with these meanings. Write the words.**

1 a space where water doesn't get in
2 the history of accidents at a place
3 gone down in the water
4 a terrible event that often kills many people
5 amazing events that almost seems impossible
6 an instrument that makes a hole in the ground
7 what's left of a car, ship, plane, etc. after a crash

WRITING
A story about a rescue

1 INPUT **Read the story. Answer the questions.**

1 Why did the boy and his friends walk across a vacant lot?
2 How long did the rescue take?
3 Why did he need to go to the hospital?
4 How did his mother feel about the rescue?

2 **Complete the story with the words.**

after | and | because | but
later | that | where

3 ANALYZE **The story has four paragraphs. Which of them ...**

a gives details about how the accident happened? ☐
b gives people's reactions to the accident? ☐
c gives a summary of the whole event? ☐
d describes how the accident was dealt with? ☐

4 PRODUCE **Think of a rescue that you know about or invent one. Write your story (200 words). Think about:**

- who was involved in the accident and the rescue.
- any special words that you will need to talk about the accident. (Use a dictionary to help you.)
- how to organize the information into paragraphs.
- how to make the story dramatic.

1 In March of 2014, 14-year-old Za'Quan Clyburn from North Carolina, USA, was rescued [1]______ he got trapped in mud.

2 Za'Quan was walking home with some friends. To save time, they walked across a vacant lot [2]______ was being prepared for a building. Za'Quan walked down a hill towards a large pool of water. He thought the ground was solid [3]______ that he could walk across it, but it was mud. He sank into it and couldn't get out. The mud went up to his chest and then almost to his chin.

3 One of his friends called 911. Firefighters arrived and started to work to get Za'Quan out. It took 24 people about half an hour to free him. Za'Quan was extremely cold and in shock, and his legs were very sore [4]______ of the pressure of the mud. An ambulance took him to the hospital, [5]______ he was kept for two days.

4 One of the firefighters said, "The outcome could have been much worse, [6]______ fortunately he came through it OK." The boy's mother said [7]______ that she was really grateful to the people who had worked so hard and risked their lives to save her son.

12 LIFE'S FIRSTS

OBJECTIVES

FUNCTIONS: expressing regret; talking about fears

GRAMMAR: phrasal verbs; *I wish / If only* + past perfect

VOCABULARY: phrasal verbs (2); nervousness and fear

Get THINKING

Watch the video and think: what is your earliest memory? How old were you?

READING

1 SPEAKING **Look at the photos. Which of these first experiences do *you* remember? Tell your partner. What other things can you remember doing for the first time?**

I remember my first day of school. I was six and I cried.

I think I can remember the first time I …

2 **Read the blog posts on the next page quickly. Which posts recall stressful moments?**

3 12.01 **Read the posts again and listen. Answer the questions.**

1 What did Emma find difficult at dinnertime?
2 What did Emma splash all over herself?
3 Why did Paul go to the hospital?
4 Why couldn't he sleep well there?
5 What was the problem that Susie had during the play?
6 How did she get the other actor to come on stage?

Train to THINK

Logical conclusions

Pay attention to conclusions in a text. Look at the ideas and arguments carefully. Do they logically lead to the conclusion?

4 **Here is a conclusion from one of the posts. Is it a logical conclusion? Why or why not?**

It was really strange that she never wrote back, but I'm sure she never got my emails.

5 **Look at the underlined conclusions. Which aren't logical? Why?**

1 Some Bradley Cooper movies are excellent. He's in *Avengers: Endgame*. It must be a good movie.
2 The chef of the restaurant around the corner is famous for his steak. Jane often eats there. Therefore, Jane often eats steak.
3 Apples are very healthy fruit. I often eat apples. I have a healthy diet.
4 Tina has fair skin and burns very easily. She's going to Brazil for a beach vacation. She needs to protect her skin from the sun.

THE FIRST TIME I …

We asked readers to tell us some of their "first times" and here are three that we liked.

My first time eating spaghetti – Italian style

My best friend in my first year at school was Italian. Her name was Caterina Ricci. We were very different, but we got along really well and went everywhere together. The first time I went to her house, we had spaghetti for dinner. I asked for a spoon, because that's how we eat spaghetti at home. When Caterina started giggling, I knew I had made a mistake. Italians only eat pasta with a spoon when it's in a broth, she told me. No big deal – watching Caterina, I tried to [1]figure out how to twirl the pasta around my fork, but all I managed to do was to splash tomato sauce all over myself. I guess I finished ten minutes later than everyone else. Nobody said anything, but I must have looked great in my white shirt covered in tomato stains! Caterina and her parents [2]moved away soon afterwards. I wrote to her a couple of times, but she didn't reply. It was really strange that she never wrote back, but I'm sure she never got my emails.

Emma

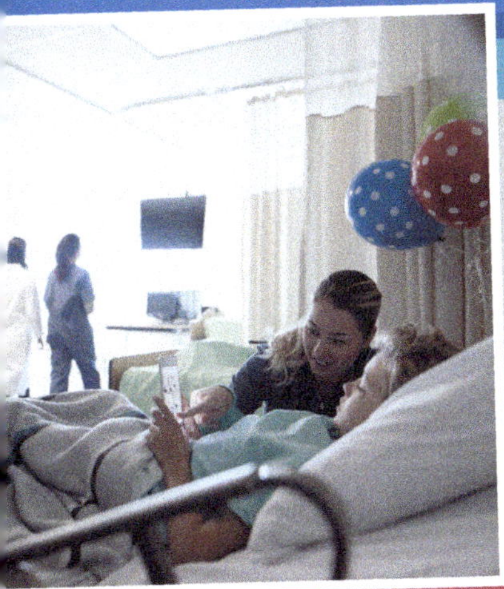

My first time in the hospital

One winter day, I went ice skating with some friends. I fell down, hit my head on the ice, and knocked myself out. My friends were worried, but I quickly [3]came to. When I told my mom and dad what had happened, they took me to the hospital. The doctor decided to keep me in overnight for some tests. There were other patients in the ward with me. One of them had had his wisdom teeth taken out. It was the first time I'd heard the words "wisdom teeth" and it sounded strange to me. I remember that I tried to talk to him, but when he spoke, I couldn't make out the words, so I couldn't understand what he was saying. I felt miserable, even though the nurses [4]took care of me and tried to [5]cheer me up. I didn't sleep well at all. It was my first night away from home and I've never forgotten it.

Paul

My first time on stage

I remember the excitement as everyone [6]put their makeup on and got into their costumes. I also remember how nervous I felt just before the curtain went up. I thought I wouldn't remember any of my lines. But in the end I didn't really have to worry about that. Everything started off well, but in the middle of the play, I [7]ran into a problem. It was in a scene with the actor who played the role of my husband. He was supposed to come on stage, but I could see him offstage talking to someone. I knew he was going to miss his entrance. He didn't come on stage, so I had to [8]make some lines up and try not to panic! It seemed like hours, although it was probably only a few seconds. Then I said, "I wonder where my husband is?" He heard me, came on stage, and we carried on with the scene. I don't think the audience noticed anything wrong.

Susie

SPEAKING

6 Work in pairs or small groups. Discuss these questions.

1 How did the various people feel about their first-time experiences?
2 Would you have felt the same in their position?
3 What personal experiences did the stories remind you of?

VOCABULARY
Phrasal verbs (2)

1 **Find the phrasal verbs in the blog posts on page 111. Match the verbs (1–8) with the definitions (a–h).**

a place (clothing, makeup) on your body so as to wear it ☐
b go to live in a different town or place ☐
c become conscious again ☐
d invent, create ☐
e watch and care for ☐
f make someone feel happy ☐
g meet a person or a problem without expecting to ☐
h understand, find the answer to ☐

2 **Complete the sentences with the correct forms of the phrasal verbs from Exercise 1.**

0 It isn't a true story – I _made_ it _up_ .
1 He is often very sad. I find it difficult to ______ him ______ .
2 Yesterday, I ______ my best friend from elementary school.
3 This question is really difficult. I can't ______ the answer.
4 We're going on vacation – can you ______ our cats while we're away, please?
5 When he fell, he was knocked unconscious, but luckily, he ______ again after a minute.
6 I don't like this place any more. I think we should ______ .
7 If you don't have a hat, please ______ some sunscreen at least.

→ workbook page 110

GRAMMAR
Phrasal verbs

3 **Look at these sentences from the text on page 111. In which ones does the object go between the two parts of the phrasal verb? Then complete the rule with the words.**

1 I had to make some lines up.
2 The nurses took care of me.
3 They tried to cheer me up.

between (x2) | separated (x2) | together

RULE: With some phrasal verbs, the two parts can't be [4]______ . They have to be [5]______ .
They ***took care of*** *me.*
Other phrasal verbs can be [6]______ . We can put an object [7]______ the two parts or after the second part.
I ***put*** *my makeup* ***on****.*
OR
I ***put on*** *my makeup.*
When we use a pronoun (*him, it*, etc.) with a phrasal verb that can be separated, it must go [8]______ the two parts of the verb.
I worked it out.
I put it on.
How do you know if a phrasal verb can be separated? Use a dictionary to look it up!
look sth up → it can be separated
look into sth → it can't be separated

4 **Put the words in order to make sentences. When there are two possible orders, write both.**

0 ago / moved / three / They / away / years
They moved away three years ago.
1 part / I'm / a / competition / in / taking
2 take / We / them / care / have to / of
3 excuse / made / an / She / up
4 joke / cheer / I / him / a / to / up / him / told
5 put / cold / It / she / jacket / was / so / her / on / that

5 SPEAKING **Complete the questions with the correct forms of the phrasal verbs. Then discuss them in small groups.**

take care of | figure out | move away
put on | run into | cheer up

1 When do you ______ nice clothes?
2 Have you ever ______ a friend in the street?
3 How do you ______ a friend if they're sad?
4 How do you ______ difficult problems?
5 Do you enjoy ______ animals or small children?
6 How would you feel if your best friend ______ ?

→ workbook page 108

LISTENING

6 SPEAKING Work in pairs. Read the quiz questions. What do you think the answers are?

QUIZ: TRANSPORTATION FIRSTS

1 Who built the first car?
A Karl Benz B Henry Ford C Gottlieb Daimler

2 Who was the first pilot to fly across the English Channel from France to England?
A Amelia Earhart B Louis Blériot C Amy Johnson

3 Who was the first person to travel into space?
A Yuri Gagarin B Neil Armstrong C Valentina Tereshkova

4 The first hot-air balloon to carry passengers, over 200 years ago ... how far did it travel?
A 9 meters B 9 km C 19 km

5 Where was the first subway line built?
A Paris B Istanbul C London

7 12.02 Listen to the same quiz on a radio show. Check your answers.

8 12.02 Listen again. Complete the notes.

1 The first car
Where? ______
When? ______

2 First flight across the English Channel
Nationality of pilot? ______
When? ______

3 First person in space
Nationality? ______
When? ______

4 First hot-air balloon flight
Where? ______
When? ______

5 Oldest subway line
Opened when? ______
Name of first line? ______

9 SPEAKING Work in pairs. Answer the questions.

1 Which of the "transportation firsts" do you think is the most important?
2 Do you think these "transportation firsts" will ever happen? If yes, when?

☐ passenger travel to the Moon
☐ non-stop flights from New York City to Sydney, Australia
☐ trains that travel at 1,000 kph

THINK values

Breaking new ground

10 Match the people (1–5) with their achievements (a–e).

1 Neil Armstrong ☐
2 Nelson Mandela ☐
3 Charles Lindbergh ☐
4 Kathryn Bigelow ☐
5 Marie Curie ☐

a was the first female director to win an Oscar.
b was the first man on the Moon.
c was the first woman to win a Nobel Prize.
d was the first man to fly alone across the Atlantic.
e was the first black president of South Africa.

11 SPEAKING Work in small groups. Discuss these questions.

1 Is it important to be the first person to do something? Why or why not?
2 What's more important: coming first (like in a competition) or just taking part?

READING

1 **From looking at these pictures, what do you think *arachnophobia* means?**

2 SPEAKING **Discuss in pairs or small groups how you or people you know react when seeing a spider?**

3 12.03 **Read and listen to the story. Mark the sentences T (true) or F (false).**

1 Over ten percent of people in the US are afraid of spiders. ☐
2 Allen thinks spiders can harm him. ☐
3 Allen didn't play the game alone. ☐
4 When he saw "Itsy" for the first time, he didn't want to continue the game. ☐
5 Allen expected that the game would not be fun. ☐
6 When Allen let the spider down, he didn't feel sorry at all. ☐
7 Allen thinks people with other fears won't find the app useful. ☐
8 Allen's sister went to the psychologist with him. ☐

4 **Do you think Allen's sister will use the app, too? Why or why not?**

THE FIRST TIME I MADE FRIENDS WITH A SPIDER

Allen was one of the 15 percent of teenagers in the US to have an extreme fear of something – also called a phobia. Allen's problem was arachnophobia: the fear of spiders. His phobia was so bad he couldn't be in a room with a spider. I asked him what he thought made spiders so terrifying. "It's the quick movement, the dark color, the legs," he said. "I couldn't look at them. I trembled if I saw one and I'd start to panic." He knew that the spiders in his house weren't dangerous and couldn't hurt him, so there was no real reason to be scared of them, but he just couldn't control his reaction.

When Allen went to see a psychologist, she told him about the Virtual Reality app *Phobia Free*. He decided to give it a try.

Allen sat with the psychologist while he played the game. I asked him how it worked. "I was asked to sit at a computer," he told me. "Then the psychologist told me I was going to meet a spider named Itsy. It felt a bit scary at first and I was glad the psychologist was with me. But when Itsy – a cartoon style animated spider – appeared, I couldn't help but smile. Itsy is fun and friendly and supports the person who has the phobia by making them kind of forget about the fear they want to overcome. And I must say I hadn't expected I would be playing an interactive game with a spider that would be so much fun! First, I was asked to help Itsy and its friends survive in difficult situations. For example, I had to help them avoid a vacuum cleaner. The game works like any computer game, but I soon noticed that I was developing an emotional link with the spiders. I really wanted to help them and when I couldn't, I felt sorry for them!"

"If I do start to feel stressed or panicky, the app has relaxation and breathing exercises that really help to calm me down. They're not just for arachnophobes like me – people who have any kind of fear or phobia will find these exercises useful."

"What's more, there's a real difference now in how I react to spiders in the real world. So, for the first time in my life, I recently touched a real spider. I saw it on my desk just in front of me. I kept really calm. I stretched out my hand and let it run over it. Wow! It wasn't as much fun as playing with Itsy, my virtual friend, but I was amazed that I was OK with it. If only I'd tried this program earlier! I might have avoided all that panic whenever I saw a spider. My sister has the same phobia and I wish she'd started this program with me, but she said the thought of it was just too frightening. Now, though, she wants to try it."

5 SPEAKING **Work in pairs or small groups. Choose a different fear and design an app for it with four or five different kinds of activities. What would they be like?**

PRONUNCIATION
Different pronunciations of *ea* Go to page 121.

GRAMMAR
I wish / If only + past perfect

6 Complete the sentences from the text on page 114. Use the correct form of the verbs. Then complete the rule.

start | try

1 If only I ______ this program earlier.
2 I wish she ______ this program with me.

> **RULE:** To express regret about the past, we can use *I wish* or *If* [3]______ + the [4]______ tense.

7 Write sentences with *I wish* ... or *If only* ... .

0 I didn't eat breakfast. Now I'm hungry.
I wish I'd eaten breakfast.
1 I didn't go to bed early. Now I'm tired.
2 I didn't ask her for her phone number.
3 Only 12 percent?! I didn't study last weekend.
4 Dad feels bad because he forgot Mom's birthday.
5 My friends are annoyed about missing the end of the movie. They fell asleep!

8 Think of three things you've done recently that you now regret. Write sentences with *I wish* ... and *If only* ... .

family | friends | vacations
money | school | shopping

→ workbook page 109

FUNCTIONS
Expressing regret

9 Put the lines in order to make a conversation.

☐ **Oliver** I'm sorry to hear that.
☐ **Oliver** What's the matter, Amelia?
☐ **Oliver** Maybe you should lie down for a few minutes.
☐ **Amelia** It was that third piece of cake. I wish I hadn't eaten it.
☐ **Amelia** That isn't a bad idea. I think I will.
☐ **Amelia** I ate too much. I feel sick.

10 SPEAKING Work in small groups. Discuss your regrets from Exercise 8 above. Make suggestions using expressions from the conversation in Exercise 9.

VOCABULARY
Nervousness and fear

11 Look at the words and phrases in bold in sentences 1–4. Match them with the pictures.

1 I was so **terrified** that I started **biting my nails**.
2 I was really **sweating**. In the end, I just **panicked** and ran out of the room.
3 When I saw the crowd in front of me, my mouth **got dry** and I started to breathe hard.
4 I started to **tremble**. In fact, I was **shaking** for about 15 minutes.

12 SPEAKING Work in pairs. What fears do the photos represent? What other things are some people afraid of?

13 Write sentences about your fears or those of people you know. Use words and phrases from Exercise 11. Then compare with a partner.

My uncle is afraid of heights. He starts to sweat, even if it's just in a movie!

→ workbook page 110

Fiction

1 12.06 **Look at the picture. What kind of place is this? Read and listen to the introduction to check your ideas.**

Bullring Kid and Country Cowboy by Louise Clover

"So are you looking forward to our holiday, Fizza?" asked her dad.
"No," thought Fizza.
"Yes, she is!" interrupted her mom. "Aren't you, darling?"
Fizza smiled falsely [...].
Fizza McIntyre is a city girl from Birmingham, UK. One year her parents hire a holiday cottage on the very small island of Sark, where there are no cars. Fizza goes along, to keep her parents happy. She doesn't know that a big adventure is going to start.

2 12.07 **Read and listen to the rest of the extract. Complete the text with the missing time expressions (a–h) below.**

a Then, lifting her nose into the air
b Later, after supper
c By the time you get back
d As she began the climb back up the hill
e For over an hour
f In five minutes
g Eventually
h For a moment

And so it was that Fizza found herself on "the island that time forgot" with absolutely nothing to do.
Her mom's voice brought her out of her dream and back to the present moment.
"Why don't you go and explore, Fizza?" said her mom. "[1] ______________________, I'll have supper ready. Oh! And get your dad a newspaper, please."
Fizza went down the hill towards the little village at the bottom. [2] ______________________ she had discovered two bicycle hire shops, three shops that sold jewelery and jugs, and a tiny post office which was also a supermarket. Fizza went up to the counter.
"Do you sell newspapers?" she asked a small grey-haired lady.
"Sorry," she said, "they haven't arrived from Guernsey today. Try tomorrow."
"What is this place?" thought Fizza. "There aren't even any newspapers!"
She thanked the lady and left the shop.
[3] ______________________, she passed a group of girls of about her age. They were chewing gum and wearing short skirts. They looked just like the "cool" girls from school, which made Fizza smile.
"Some things never change," she thought, "wherever you go." And she began to run back towards the cottage.
[4] ______________________, Fizza and her dad practiced judo in the field behind the cottage.
[5] ______________________, they threw one another onto the grass until Imran admitted defeat and went inside to play a game of cards with Rubel.
As the sun began to drop down from the sky like a great big orange, Fizza continued to practice her judo moves. [6] ______________________, she got tired and stopped. She looked out at the dark grey sea and breathed in deeply. And for the first time since she had arrived on Sark, she found herself listening. She could hear the birds singing goodnight to each other, and the sound of sheep bells and a boat in the distance.
[7] ______________________, she breathed in deeply and she found that the evening air of Sark smelled sweet. It was completely different from the heavy city smell of her much-loved Birmingham. Such beauty suddenly made Fizza McIntyre feel alive and she decided to show the island how good she felt.
"Goodnight, Sark!" she shouted as she jumped high in the air and then fell on the grass.
Laughing at herself for being silly, she picked herself up and turned to go indoors, but immediately she came to a stop.
Sitting in a tree beside the cottage was a red-haired boy who looked about the same age as her.
[8] ______________________ they stared at one another until her attention was taken by a small brown rabbit that ran past her. She took her eyes away from the boy for just a few seconds and during this time he completely disappeared.

3 **Read the rest of the extract again. Mark the statements T (true) or F (false).**

1 The store on the island never has newspapers. ☐
2 Fizza sees some girls who remind her of her school. ☐
3 Fizza and her father do judo together. ☐
4 Fizza thinks that the air on the island is like the air at home. ☐
5 She shouts, "Goodnight, Sark" because the island made her feel good. ☐
6 The boy she sees is chasing a rabbit. ☐

4 SPEAKING **Think about these questions. Then discuss your answers with other students.**

Imagine you can travel somewhere that's completely different from where you live.

1 Where would you choose to go? Why?
2 What would you miss most about where you live now?

WRITING
A story about a bad decision

1 INPUT **Read the story. What was Pauline's bad decision, according to the writer?**

2 **Find sentences in the story with these meanings. How are the underlined phrases expressed in the story?**

1 <u>Pauline regretted the fact that she'd gone</u> to the big university.
2 <u>It's a shame that you didn't tell</u> us.
3 <u>I think it's a shame that she didn't tell</u> her parents.
4 <u>It isn't good that Pauline didn't make</u> her own decision.

3 ANALYZE **The story has four paragraphs. Which of them ...**

a is about a decision that the person made?
b gives background information about the person?
c gives the writer's thoughts about the whole situation?
d explains the effects of the decision?

4 PRODUCE **Think of a (true or invented) story about a bad decision. Write your story (200 words). Think about:**

- who the person is / was.
- the situation the person was in which meant that he/she had to make a decision.
- the decision that the person made.
- what happened after making the decision.
- what you or the person felt about it all afterwards.

ABOUT BLOG LATEST POSTS ARCHIVES

LEARNING FROM EXPERIENCE?

We asked readers to tell us stories about bad decisions they or people they know have made.

Here's this week's story.

1 A friend of mine has a sister, Pauline, who's six years older than him. She was always good at school, but all she really wanted to do was to help her parents in their small store and then perhaps take it over when they were too old to run it.

2 Pauline's parents, however, really wanted her to go to college, so she spent two years at community college working incredibly hard, studying for an exam so that she could go to a big university in another city. She passed and a few months later she left home to start studying there.

3 From the beginning, Pauline wished she hadn't gone to the university. She hated it. She'd been a good student in high school and did well at the community college, but the courses at the university were much harder. She didn't make many friends either, so she was lonely and homesick. After six months, she asked her parents to let her leave and come home. They were very surprised when she said that she'd never wanted to go to college. "If only you'd told us!" they said. "But I didn't want to disappoint you," was her answer.

4 Now Pauline is working at the store and she's very happy. I wish she'd told her parents that college wasn't what she wanted – then she wouldn't have wasted six months of her life. Pauline should have made her own decision.

TOWARDS B2 First for Schools

READING AND USE OF ENGLISH

Gapped text

→ workbook page 115

1 You are going to read about someone travelling abroad for the first time. Six sentences have been removed from the text. Choose from the sentences (A–G) the one that fits each gap (1–6). There is one extra sentence that you do not need to use.

I've never really enjoyed travelling very much. The idea of leaving the comfort of my own bed to sleep somewhere else has never appealed to me. And when you add in things like the food and not being understood, the thought of leaving my hometown fills me with terror. I did go away on a school trip once, when I was eight, for two nights. My mother tells me I quite enjoyed the experience. 1 ______ There must be a reason why I can't remember anything positive about it.

So for 28 years I'd managed to lead a life that kept me happily at home. A few nights in hotels for work had been the worst I'd had to go through. Then, one day, my boss called me in. He shook my hand. He was smiling from one ear to the other. 2 ______ 'Paul!' he announced. 'You've been promoted.' I should have been happy, I suppose, but something in the back of my mind was telling me this wasn't 100 percent good news. 3 ______ 'Of course, you'll need extra training. I've booked you on a course at head office in Linz. Your flight's on Monday.'

I started to feel dizzy. I had to hold on to the table to stop myself from falling. My boss patted me on the back.

'Great news, eh?' he smiled. Then he left the room.

So that was it. Just when my professional life had got better, the rest of my life was over. No one had ever survived an aeroplane flight, had they? 4 ______ I wasn't so sure. I spent the weekend making my final farewells as Monday morning got closer.

5 ______ Before I knew it, my taxi had left me at the airport. Somehow I made my way to the check-in desk. I lifted my suitcase onto the conveyor belt and walked through airport security to the lounge. I have no idea how I knew what to do. I guess that because I'd seen it so many times in films, it was programmed into my mind.

The flight was only two hours. 6 ______ I tried to read a book, but I couldn't. I tried listening to my MP3 player – I'd chosen some relaxing music especially – but it sounded like it was being played by an orchestra of three-year-olds. Every sound the plane made sent my imagination spinning out of control. Was that the sound of the wing falling off? Was that a bird being sucked through an engine? Was that the noise of wheels hitting the runway? Yes, it was. We had landed.

Somehow we'd arrived. I wanted to grab my fellow travellers and celebrate the fact that we were still alive, but they were all busy getting their luggage from the overhead lockers. So I celebrated on my own.
But then I remembered: unless I wanted to spend the rest of my life in Austria, I still had to fly back!

A What wasn't right about this?
B My family and friends tried to assure me that of course they had.
C I thought that it was never going to end.
D And then the day I had been dreading arrived.
E Would I ever see my wife again?
F It wasn't long before I found out why.
G That certainly isn't what my memory tells me.

TEST YOURSELF UNITS 11 & 12

VOCABULARY

1 Complete the sentences with the words / phrases in the list. There are four extra words / phrases.

survived | afraid | illogical | figure out | rescued | panicked | informal | dangerous
hang out | run into | coming to | irresponsible | impatient | made up

1 After she hit her head, she slowly started ______ .
2 I can't come climbing with you. No way! I'm ______ of heights.
3 The firefighter ______ the cat from the tree.
4 The show didn't go very well – I ______ when I walked on stage, and then I forgot what I wanted to say.
5 Luckily, everyone ______ the plane crash last night.
6 Don't be so ______ . It'll be your turn soon.
7 They ______ that story. There is no way that it is true.
8 I can't ______ the answer to this question. Can you help me?
9 It was very ______ of you to go swimming during the storm.
10 When I'm in town, I often ______ people I know.

/10

GRAMMAR

2 Complete the sentences with the words / phrases in the list. There are two extra words / phrases.

I wish | if | only | such | feel like | afford | so | in order to

1 It was ______ a loud noise that everybody in the street heard it.
2 He jumped into the lake ______ rescue the boy.
3 I don't ______ going swimming. It's too cold.
4 He can't ______ to buy that computer game. He owes Tom some money.
5 Everyone laughs at my hair. If ______ I hadn't dyed it green!
6 ______ you'd waited for me. Then this wouldn't have happened.

3 Find and correct the mistake in each sentence.

1 It's a complicated problem. We need to figure out it.
2 I decided going out this evening.
3 I'm such hungry! I'll have to eat something now.
4 They're going to cover the hole so to prevent future accidents.
5 It was so bad a movie that we left before it had finished.
6 After the accident, my dad promised wearing a seat belt in the future.

/12

FUNCTIONAL LANGUAGE

4 Choose the correct words.

1 A The police want to increase the fine to $1,000 *for* / *to* stop people from driving so fast.
B I think that's *so* / *such* a good idea.
2 A What's the *shame* / *matter*, Erika?
B I'm feeling a bit sick. I wish I *hadn't* / *haven't* eaten all that cake.
3 A Let's have a book sale *in* / *on* order to make some money for the school.
B That's not a bad *matter* / *idea*.
4 A His headache was *so* / *such* bad that he couldn't concentrate on the exam.
B I'm sorry to hear *this* / *that*.

/8

MY SCORE /30

22–30 | 10–21 | 0–9

PRONUNCIATION

UNIT 7

Intonation – inviting, accepting, and refusing invitations

1 7.05 **Read and listen to the dialogue.**

Max Hi, Gina! I'm organizing a hiking trip. Why don't you come along?

Gina Thank you, Max. I'd love to. When are you going?

Max Next Saturday. We're going to climb Mount Sunrise. How about bringing some friends?

Gina That's a great idea! Oh … I'm already going out on Saturday. What a shame. I'm sorry, Max.

2 7.05 **Make a note of the two invitations and the sentences where Gina accepts and refuses the invitation. What happens to Max and Gina's voice in each case? Listen again and check.**

3 7.06 **Listen, repeat, and practice.**

UNIT 8

Intonation – expressing surprise

1 8.06 **Read and listen to the dialogue.**

Jackson You're not going to believe this.

Maryanne Tell me.

Jackson School's closed for the rest of the term!

Maryanne What?

Jackson The police said there was an urgent situation but didn't give any details.

Maryanne That's awful!

Jackson And the principal said she's extremely sorry, but there's nothing she can do!

Maryanne Really?

2 8.06 **Listen again and write down all of the words that are stressed.**

3 8.07 **Listen, repeat, and practice.**

UNIT 9

Moving word stress

1 9.02 **Read and listen to the dialogues.**

1 A Do you know the mystery of Amelia Earhart?
B Yes – her disappearance is very mysterious!

2 A Wow! That's a great photograph.
B Thanks! I'm really into photography.

3 A If we go to this summer camp, we can do the course on navigation.
B But I already know how to navigate.

2 **Find the stressed syllables in the words in blue. Say the two words in blue in each dialogue.**

3 9.03 **Listen, repeat, and practice.**

UNIT 10

Short and long vowel sounds: /ɪ/ – /iː/ and /ɑ/ – /oʊ/

1 10.03 **Read and listen to the dialogues.**

Mrs. Green We all need good self esteem. But what does it mean? Tim?

Tim It's a lot of things, Mrs. Green. But it's really important to feel happy to be as we are.

Mr. Ross So, do you copy your favorite pop stars? Do you wear the same clothes, Rose?

Rose Mr. Ross! I follow pop stars – but I don't wear the same clothes! I'm not a clone.

2 **Say the words with the *short* /ɪ/ and the *long* /iː/ sounds. How does your mouth change shape? Say the words with the *short* /ɑ/ and the *long* /oʊ/ sounds. How does your mouth change shape now?**

3 10.04 **Listen, repeat, and practice.**

UNIT 11

Strong and weak forms: /tuː/ and /tə/

1 11.02 **Read and listen to the dialogue.**

Steve Hi, Jane! It's good to see you. What have you been up to?

Jane I've been traveling. I've been to so many places, I couldn't name them all!

Steve Wow, that's exciting. Did you go to Germany?

Jane Well … that's one place I didn't get to. I went to France and Spain, though.

2 **Say the words in blue with the weak form of *to*. Now say the words in red in the strong form.**

3 11.03 **Listen, repeat, and practice.**

UNIT 12

Different pronunciations of *ea*

1 12.04 **Read and listen to the dialogue.**

Teacher Has everyone read the article about healthy living?

Jean I have, sir. From the research, I learned that we have to take care of ourselves from an early age.

Teacher Yes, it would appear that every year counts. Are there any more ideas?

Heather Eating and sleeping well is really important, Mr. Heath.

Teacher Great answer. Now let's take a break!

2 **How many different pronunciations of the *ea* spelling are there? Say the highlighted words.**

3 12.05 **Listen, repeat, and practice.**

GET IT RIGHT!

UNIT 7

make vs. *let*

Learners sometimes confuse *make* and *let* in phrases such as *let me know*.

✓ *You were on TV and you didn't* ***let*** *us know!*

✗ *You were on TV and you didn't ~~make~~ us know!*

Complete the sentences with the correct form of *make* or *let*.

0 There are spacious seats, which will ___make___ you feel very comfortable.

1 ___________ me help you with that bag. It looks really heavy.

2 The band came on stage late. They ___________ us wait over an hour.

3 That TV documentary about diet and health really ___________ me think about doing more exercise.

4 Mom, can you write a note to my teacher to ___________ her know why I won't be in class tomorrow?

5 It's so important to ___________ people aware of the disease so that we can raise money to help prevent it.

6 It was very kind of you to ___________ us stay over, Mrs. Johnson. Thanks very much for having us!

UNIT 8

say vs. *tell*

Learners sometimes confuse *say* and *tell*.

The meaning of *say* and *tell* is exactly the same, but we use them differently.

We *tell someone* (*something*) and we *say something* (*to someone*).

✓ *I didn't* ***say anything to*** *my brother about it.*

✗ *I didn't ~~tell anything to~~ my brother about it.*

We can also use a *that* clause immediately after *tell*, but not after *say*.

✓ ***Tell her that*** *I'll call her.*

✗ *~~Say her that~~ I'll call her.*

There are some collocations we can use with *tell* that don't follow the above rules: we can *tell a lie / the truth / a story*.

Complete each of these sentences with the correct form of *say* or *tell*.

0 Everybody ___said___ something about himself and so did I.

1 I have to ___________ that this is a great piece of writing. Well done!

2 You're going to have to ___________ him that you can't play in Saturday's game. You're injured.

3 ___________ us the story of how you met.

4 Did he ___________ why he lied?

5 My Mom ___________ that we were going to move to a new house.

6 I'd like to ___________ thank you for all your help this year.

7 I knew that he ___________ the truth.

UNIT 9
Modals of deduction in the present

It is a common error to use *can* as a present modal of deduction, where *could* is required. In the negative, however, it is possible to use *can't* as well as *couldn't*.

✓ *I'm not sure why they decided not to buy tickets to see the band, but it **could be** due to lack of money.*

✗ *I'm not sure why they decided not to buy tickets to see the band, but it ~~can be~~ due to lack of money.*

✓ *The reason **can't be** a lack of interest.*

Which of these sentences are correct and which are incorrect? Rewrite the incorrect ones.

0 Where's John? He can be at home.
Where's John? He could be at home.

1 **A** Do you have a better idea for how to get there?
B Well, I think another route can be better.

______

2 **A** Is his car broken down?
B It can be. The man looks like he might be waving for us to stop.

______

3 **A** How does that car go so fast?
B It can be because it's so light. Just a guess!

______

4 **A** What do you think is going to happen in the game?
B They could still win or maybe it'll be a tie.

______

5 **A** Is Dad still at work?
B The car's outside. He can't be at work.

______

6 **A** Who made the complaint?
B It could be Nick – he didn't think there was a problem.

______

UNIT 10
Future continuous vs. simple future

Learners often confuse the future continuous with the simple future.
We use the future continuous to talk about events that will be in the process of happening at some time in the future.

✓ *This time next week **I'll be sitting** on the beach in Florida.*

✗ *This time next week ~~I'll sit~~ on the beach in Florida.*

Decide if the sentences can be written in the future continuous. If so, rewrite them using this tense. What's the difference in meaning between the simple future and future continuous form in these cases?

0 When you get to the station, I'll wait for you at the main entrance.
When you get to the station, I'll be waiting for you at the main entrance.

1 This time next year, we'll be in college and we'll live away from home.

______

2 I'll take a look at my schedule and see if I'm free on the 5th.

______

3 This time next week, I'll take my final exam.

______

4 Some people think that tablets will soon replace laptops.

______

5 I'll play hockey when you arrive at the station tomorrow, but Chloë can meet you.

______

6 I think you'll have a good time when you go to Spain.

______

UNIT 11
Verb patterns

Learners sometimes make errors with verb patterns, using *to* + infinitive, when it should be a gerund and vice versa.

✓ *I **don't mind going** home first.*

✗ *I ~~don't mind to go~~ home first.*

Which of these sentences are correct and which are incorrect? Rewrite the incorrect ones.

0 He's always had problems to focus on one task.
He's always had problems focusing on one task.

1 Do you need more time finishing your work?

2 Lately, I've been spending a lot of time to watch TV.

3 I need to start working on my essay as soon as possible.

4 It was an intense movie, but we enjoyed to learn about history.

5 It's best studying new vocabulary regularly.

6 I had real difficulties downloading this app, but I got it eventually.

UNIT 12
Phrasal verbs

Learners sometimes avoid using phrasal verbs, using single, often Latinate, verbs instead. Using phrasal verbs can make you sound more natural and increase the variety of your English.

✓✓ *Students were **put up** in hotels.*

✓ *Students were **accommodated** in hotels.*

Replace the verbs in bold with phrasal verbs from the list.

put up with | put on | put up (x2) | put off

0 Before I went to the beach, I **applied** sunscreen.
Before I went to the beach, I put on sunscreen.

1 Our family has agreed to **host** a foreign student for a month during the summer.

2 One advantage of taking the train is that you don't have to **tolerate** traffic jams.

3 I don't get to exercise so much any more and I'm worried about **gaining** weight.

4 Good news! We're going to have to **postpone** today's test until next Friday.

5 We **displayed** posters to advertise the event.

STUDENT A

UNIT 7, PAGE 72

Student A

1 Invite your partner to do these things with you. Then, add one more idea of your own.
  - Watch a soccer game at the local field.
  - Meet some of your friends and go to the shopping mall.

2 Accept or refuse your partner's invitations.

STUDENT B

UNIT 7, PAGE 72

Student B

1 Accept or refuse your partner's invitations.

2 Invite your partner to do these things with you. Then, add one more idea of your own.
   - Watch a horror movie at your place.
   - Go for a long walk in the mountains.

Acknowledgements

The authors and publishers acknowledge the following sources of copyright material and are grateful for the permissions granted. While every effort has been made, it has not always been possible to identify the sources of all the material used, or to trace all copyright holders. If any omissions are brought to our notice, we will be happy to include the appropriate acknowledgements on reprinting and in the next update to the digital edition, as applicable.

Key: W= Welcome; U = Unit.

Text

U8: The Clink Restaurant for the text about the restaurant. Copyright © The Clink Restaurant. Reproduced with kind permission; **U9:** Cambridge University Press for the text from *Wild Country* by Margaret Johnson. Copyright © 2008 Cambridge University Press. Reproduced with permission; **U12:** Cambridge University Press for the text from *Bullring Kid and Country Cowboy* by Louise Clover. Copyright © 2009, 2010 Cambridge University Press. Reproduced with permission.

Photography

All the photographs are sourced from Getty Images.

U7: Wavebreakmedia/iStock/Getty Images Plus; JAG Images/Corbis; SolStock/E+; Boston Globe; Chagin/iStock/Getty Images Plus; Samantha Mitchell/Corbis/VCG; Nabila Hossain/EyeEm; ferozeea/iStock/Getty Images Plus; Singh_Lens/iStock/Getty Images Plus; Gallo Images; Roger de la Harpe/Gallo Images/Getty Images Plus; Michael Runkel/robertharding/Getty Images Plus; Robert Niedring/Alloy; **U8:** Peter Dazeley/The Image Bank; Michaela Begsteiger; Steven Puetzer/Photographer's Choice; sturti/E+; Radius Images; Fabian von Poser; Michael Cilliers/EyeEm; André Dias Duarte/Moment; filo/E+; DGLimages/iStock/Getty Images Plus; rabbit75_ist/iStock/Getty Images Plus; Gonzalo Azumendi/The Image Bank/Getty Images Plus; Highwaystarz-Photography/iStock/Getty Images Plus; jacoblund/iStock/Getty Images Plus; KatarzynaBialasiewicz/iStock/Getty Images Plus; GoodLifeStudio/E+; **U9:** Keystone/Hulton Archive/Getty Images Plus; Marco Simoni/Cultura; Buddy Mays/Corbis Unreleased; ktsimage/iStock/Getty Images Plus; MarkGillow/E+; Universal History Archive/Universal Images Group; Luis Dias/500px Prime; Dimitris66/DigitalVision Vectors; SVF2/Universal Images Group; KARL-JOSEF Hildenbrand/DPA; **U10:** JGI/Tom Grill; lzf/iStock/Getty Images Plus; payphoto/iStock/Getty Images Plus; petekarici/iStock/Getty Images Plus; DjelicS/E+; VioletaStoimenova/E+; Witthaya Prasongsin/EyeEm; MarioGuti/E+; andresr/E+; Bloomberg; Jose Luis Pelaez Inc/DigitalVision; Prasit photo/Moment; shapecharge/E+; kali9/E+; momcilog/E+; Matt Cardy/Stringer/Getty Images News; **U11:** Photobos/iStock Editorial; BSIP/Universal Images Group; Tashi-Delek/E+; Linh Pham/Getty Images News; Eitan Abramovich/AFP; technotr/E+; Kelvin Murray/Stone; Sean Gladwell/Moment; HadelProductions/E+; Sunrise@dawn Photography/Moment; **U12:** SDI Productions/E+; yaoinlove/iStock/Getty Images Plus; Caiaimage; Guido Mieth/Moment; Halfdark; Hero Images; Carlos Mayo/EyeEm; Iuliia Safronova/iStock/Getty Images Plus; jsteck/E+; Andrew Merry/Moment; Byronsdad/E+; Peter McBride; Greg Bajor/Moment.

The following photographs are sourced from other sources/libraries.

U8: David Alary/Shutterstock; © The Clink Restaurant; **U9:** Mostardi Photography/Alamy Stock Photo; Cecilia Bleasdale for the image of 'The Dress', Copyright © Cecilia Bleasdale. Reproduced with permission; **U10:** Richard Levine/Alamy Stock Photo; **U11:** WENN Rights Ltd/Alamy Stock Photo; **U12:** Bernd Tschakert Photography/Alamy Stock Photo; Cambridge University Press for the front cover image of *Bullring Kid and Country Cowboy* (2009) by Louise Clover. Reproduced with permission of Cambridge University Press.

Cover photography by Mustafagull/E+/Getty Images; George Pachantouris/Moment/Getty Images.

Illustrations

U12: Martin Sanders; **U9, U11:** Daniella Geremia; **U9:** Ben Scruton; **U9, U12:** Mark Ruffle; **U8:** Graham Kennedy; **U9, U11:** Adam Linley.

Documentary Video Stills

All the stills are sourced from Getty Images.

U7: Sunday Times/Gallo Images; **U8:** damircudic/Creatas Video; Samuel Magal/Photolibrary Video; **U9:** itsskin/Creatas Video; **U10:** Visual_Bricks/Creatas Video+/Getty Images Plus; **U11:** ITN; footagefactory/Image Bank Film; **U12:** Yamato1987/Creatas Video.

Audio production by CityVox, New York.

Vlog & Grammar Rap Video Stills: Silversun Media Group.

WORKBOOK
with Digital Pack

3

CEFR
B1+

AMERICAN THINK

SECOND EDITION

Herbert Puchta,
Jeff Stranks &
Peter Lewis-Jones
with Clare Kennedy

CAMBRIDGE
UNIVERSITY PRESS

This page is intentionally left blank.

CONTENTS

7 BREAKING AWAY

Grammar rap! ▶18

GRAMMAR

make / let and *be allowed to* → SB p.68

1 ★☆☆ Complete the sentences with *make* or *let*.

Here is what life is like at summer camp. Some things are great – others, not so much!

1 They __________ us watch TV every evening until 10:30.
2 They __________ us clean our shoes every day.
3 They __________ us clean the things in our room at the end of every day.
4 They __________ us check our phones twice a day.
5 They __________ us spend our free time in our rooms.
6 They __________ us take a cold shower every day.
7 They __________ us sleep late on Saturdays and Sundays.
8 They __________ us eat vegetables with every meal.

2 ★★☆ Rewrite the sentences using *makes, doesn't make, lets,* or *doesn't let*.

0 **Mom** You have to do the dishes after dinner.
Mom makes me do the dishes after dinner.
1 **Dad** You can stay out later on Saturdays.
____
2 **Mom** You can't play loud music in the house.
____
3 **Mom** You don't have to clean your room.
____
4 **Mom** You don't have to get up early on Sundays.
____
5 **Dad** You can't drive my car.
____
6 **Dad** You have to take out the trash.
____
7 **Dad** You can invite friends over on the weekend.
____

3 ★★★ Look at the signs. Rewrite them using *You're (not) allowed to*.

0 *You're not allowed to bike here.*

1 ______________________________

2 ______________________________

3 ______________________________

4 ______________________________

5 ______________________________

6 ______________________________

7 ______________________________

4 ★★★ Complete the sentences so that they are true for you.

1 I'm not allowed to ______________
2 My friends never let me ______________
3 At school, we're allowed to ______________
4 Our teacher doesn't let us ______________
5 I don't like it when someone makes me ______________
6 It isn't fair to make someone ______________

5 ★★★ **Make questions using the prompts and *make / let / be allowed to*.**

0 parents / you / help with the housework?
Do your parents make you help with the housework?

1 teachers / you / do homework every night?
______

2 you / send messages in class?
______

3 school / you / go into any room you want?
______

4 parents / you / sleep as long as you like?
______

5 you / eat anything you want at home?
______

6 parents / you / stay out after midnight?
______

6 ★★★ **Write your answers to the questions in Exercise 5.**

0 ______
1 ______
2 ______
3 ______
4 ______
5 ______
6 ______

be / get used to

→ SB p.69

7 ★☆☆ **Match the parts of the sentences.**

1 When we went to Boston, it took us time ☐
2 She was a bit nervous because ☐
3 It isn't always easy ☐
4 At first, Mom didn't like working from home, ☐
5 My brother is learning Arabic and he has to ☐
6 When my sister joined the police, she ☐
7 He didn't like the cat at first because ☐
8 Can I have a knife and fork, please? ☐

a she wasn't used to traveling alone.
b get used to writing from right to left.
c had to get used to wearing a uniform.
d to get used to the local accent.
e he was used to having dogs at home.
f I'm not used to using chopsticks.
g but then she got used to it.
h to get used to life in a different country.

8 ★★☆ **Complete the sentences with *be used to* or *get used to* and the correct form of a verb from the list.**

eat | go | live | (not) hug | read

1 Before I went to China, I ______ with a knife and fork, but then I ______ with chopsticks.
2 Back home, when I had a job, I ______ to work by train, so I had to ______ to work by bus in China.
3 I also had to ______ people very much – it wasn't easy because in my country, we ______ our family and friends a lot!
4 And of course in my language, I ______ things in the Roman alphabet, but when I started to learn Chinese, I had to ______ Chinese characters.
5 So now I ______ in China, but I won't live here forever – in two years, I'll go back home, I think.

GET IT RIGHT!

be used to vs. *get used to*

Learners have difficulty telling the difference between *be used to something* and *get used to something*.

We use *be used to* to say that we are familiar with something now.

✓ *My friends in Spain find it strange that we eat dinner at 6 p.m., but it's normal for us. We're used to it.*
✗ *My friends in Spain find it strange that we eat dinner at 6 p.m., but it's normal for us. We get used to it.*

We use *get used to* to talk about the process of becoming familiar with something over time.

✓ *When I first came to the US, I found it strange to eat dinner at 6 p.m., but after a while I got used to it.*
✗ *When I first came to the US, I found it strange to eat dinner at 6 p.m., but after a while I am used to it.*

Circle the correct words.

1 Swimming practice was hard at first, but I *am / got* used to it eventually.
2 It's easy to get up at 8 a.m., now that I*'m / got* used to it.
3 I finally *am / got* used to the rain in Seattle after a few months.
4 At first, he didn't like his new school, but after a few weeks he *is / got* used to it.
5 Ciara didn't understand her new Spanish teacher, but now she *is / got* used to her accent.
6 *Are / Did* you get used to the food there eventually?

VOCABULARY
Phrasal verbs (1)

→ SB p.68

1 ★☆☆ Match the verbs (1–8) with their definitions (a–h).

1 turn down
2 take up
3 show up
4 give up
5 keep on
6 find out
7 end up
8 set off

a stop doing something (often a bad habit)
b discover
c start a journey
d refuse or say no to someone
e begin (a hobby or new subject)
f arrive at a place after a long time (after some time or effort)
g continue
h arrive at a place (often late or unexpectedly)

2 ★★☆ Complete the sentences with the correct forms of the phrasal verbs in Exercise 1.

1 They were so late! We agreed to meet at 7:30 but they didn't ___________ until 8:15!
2 We started playing at three in the afternoon, and we ___________ playing until it got dark.
3 Sam was so happy when he ___________ that he'd won the competition.
4 After a while trying to find the house, we ___________ getting there too late for the party!
5 I'm really sorry but I have to ___________ your invitation. I'm busy on Saturday.
6 We ___________ at eight in the morning and by noon, we were at the beach!
7 The exam was too hard! After 20 minutes I ___________ and left the room.
8 My dad was getting bored at home, so he ___________ golf and now he's out all the time.

Personality

→ SB p.71

3 ★☆☆ Complete the puzzle.

1 It was very ___________ of you to offer to help.
2 I didn't like him – he was very ___________ .
3 I like her – she's a very ___________ person.
4 It's "me, me, me" all the time – she's so ___________ .
5 I like her smile – it's so ___________ and welcoming.
6 He always says things nicely – he's very ___________ .
7 Please don't laugh at me – it's very ___________ .
8 She won't come and talk to you – she's too ___________ .

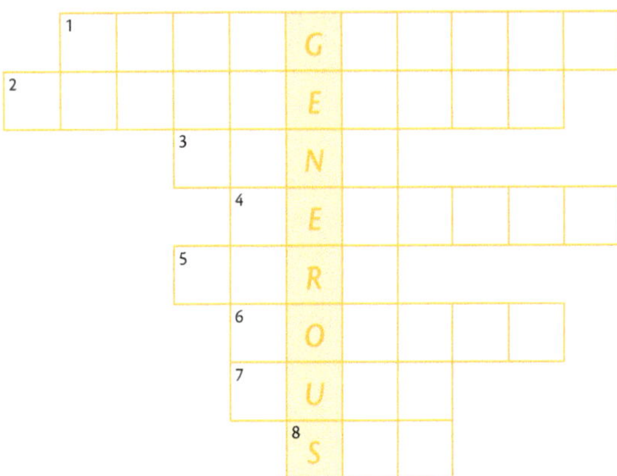

4 ★★☆ Complete the sentences with personality adjectives. Start each adjective with the first letter of the person's name.

1 Layla is ___________

3 Simon is ___________

2 Chris is ___________

4 Gisella is ___________

WordWise: Phrases with *all*

→ SB p.69

5 ★★☆ Complete the sentences with the correct phrase with *all* from the list.

all day | all I'm saying | all the same
for all I know | once and for all | after all

1 Of course I'll help you. ___________, you're my friend!
2 I've been working on this problem ___________ – I'm tired!
3 A Who's that guy over there?
B I have no idea. He could be anyone, ___________ .
4 You've asked me that question five times! ___________, I don't know – OK?
5 Look, I know it's your favorite movie. ___________ is that I didn't like it.
6 Well, we can go to the gym or to the park. It's ___________ to me.

REFERENCE

Phrasal verbs (1)

- end up
- find out
- keep on
- turn down
- give up
- set off
- show up
- take up

Positive
calm, generous, kind, polite, warm, thoughtful

Neutral
lively, shy

Negative
cold, rude, selfish, unfriendly

PHRASES WITH ALL

- after all
- all day
- all the same
- all the time
- all (we're) saying (is)
- first of all
- for all I know
- once and for all

VOCABULARY *EXTRA*

1 **Mark the phrasal verbs in bold positive (✓), negative (✗), or neutral (N). Sometimes there is more than one correct answer.**

1 I spent all my money on clothes. They were all so cool, I just **got carried away.** ______

2 Asia often **lets** us **down**. She agrees to help and then doesn't show up. ______

3 We **look up to** Miss Jenkins. Everyone respects her. ______

4 Jacob thinks he's really important and **looks down on** other people. ______

5 The cost of my gym pass has increased, but I don't want to give it up. I'll just have to **put up with it**! ______

6 I can **rely on** Johnny because I know I can trust him. ______

2 **Put the words in order to make sentences.**

1 us / Thomas / to / we / on / help / always / rely / can
______

2 on / down / classmates / Maya / her / looks /
______

3 someone / teenagers / up / they / look / need / to / can
______

4 I / my / never / let / friends / down
______

5 with / mistakes / teacher / the / up / won't / put / spelling
______

6 game / Harry / away / with / got / carried / the
______

3 **Complete the sentences so that they are true for you.**

1 You can rely on me to ______

2 I sometimes get carried away when ______

3 My parents won't put up with ______

4 The person I look up to most is ______ because ______

DAN'S DAILY Discussions

Last week, I asked you, my readers, to think about people and [a]stereotypes. I knew I could rely on you to send in some interesting ideas! This is what you came up with. I call this collection: ________________.

1 At the end of the day, we're all human beings, and that's that. The best way to [b]challenge stereotypes is just by being who you are and accepting others as they are. If we learn to do that, then we'll all get along better with each other. *Lia Cox*

2 I think people are all the same, really. We're born in different places and we have different cultures. We don't all look the same or speak the same language. But people are all the same, although we differ in hundreds of ways. That's what makes life so interesting! Let's celebrate our [c]diversity! *George Henderson*

3 Wasn't it the American writer Ernest Hemingway who said that everyone's life ends sooner or later? It's just how we live and how we die that [d]distinguish us from each other. *Mike Gillespie*

4 I think it's beautiful that everyone is different. If we were all the same, life would be very boring. We should allow everyone to live their lives in their own way. *Jenny Price*

5 My grandma always said that people are people. She always treated everyone in the same way and that's something we should all try to do. Too often, we let a person's appearance [e]influence what we think of them. We shouldn't look down on anyone because, in the end, we are all human beings and we should treat everyone equally. *Sarah White*

6 I forget who said, "When it's dark, we're all the same." I think this quotation is trying to remind us that people are basically all the same. It doesn't matter if someone is tall or short, young or old. We shouldn't judge people on their clothes, color of their skin, what they believe, or their culture. The main point is, though, that we all need to learn to put up with people who are different from us. That's the real problem. *Agata Morris*

7 The American president John F. Kennedy said that we share a lot of things. We all live on the same planet, and we all breathe the same air. We think about our children's future. And we'll all die one day. The world would be a better place if we remembered this [f]quotation. JFK said a lot of wise things and I look up to him for this. *Paul Gibson*

8 Someone once said that there are two kinds of people: those who divide the world into two kinds of people, and those who don't. How true this is! *Janie Smith*

9 A friend of mine who had white hair when she was only 20 said, "You laugh at me because I'm different. I laugh at you because you're all the same!" *Mandy Atkins*

READING

1 **Read the comments on the blog page. Choose the title you think best fits the page.**

A We are all the same
B The same but different
C Everyone is different

2 **Match the highlighted words in the blog page (a–f) with the definitions (1–6).**

1 one or a few sentences taken from a book or play, or that were said by someone else ☐
2 differences ☐
3 fixed and often wrong ideas of what a person is like ☐
4 question if something is true ☐
5 recognize differences between two things ☐
6 change what people think ☐

3 **Each of the writers agrees with one of the opinions below. Write the numbers (1–9) in the correct column.**

We need to learn to accept each other.	Diversity is great and should be celebrated.
______	______
______	______
______	______
______	______
______	______

4 CRITICAL THINKING **Underline the sentence or phrase that best summarizes the writer's opinion in each comment.**

1 *we're all human beings and that's that*

DEVELOPING Writing

A blog about a different country

1 INPUT **Read the blog and check (✓) the photos of the things that Francesca mentions.**

A ☐

B ☐

C ☐

D ☐

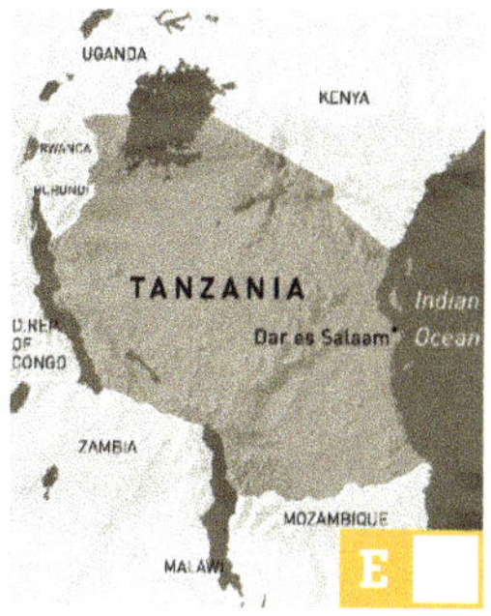

E ☐

BLOG ABOUT NEWS ADVICE GALLERY CONTACT

Here I am in Tanzania! We arrived a few weeks ago and we'll be staying for two years, so I'm going to write about my experiences – here's my first post.

Dar es Salaam! [1]__________, I love the place. It's wonderfully warm, but it gets humid sometimes and then you feel uncomfortable, but I'm slowly getting used to that. At this time of year, it rains every day for about an hour, usually in the afternoon. Sometimes it rains really hard! But when it stops, you get the wonderful smell of grass after summer rain.

[2]__________, some things are different. Dar es Salaam isn't the capital, but it's a big city with over four million people living here – very different from our little town back home. There's one thing I'll never get used to: the huge traffic jams. It takes ages to drive anywhere. There's a cool atmosphere in the city: it has an amazing cultural mix and the people are warm, friendly, and calm – nobody ever seems to be in a hurry!

[3]__________ there's the food – it's all new for me, but delicious. My favorite is *Ndizi Kaanga* – that's fried green bananas.

[4]__________ I like most: it's the way people always shake hands when they meet. You must shake everyone's hand – even if there are 20 people – and you should start with the oldest person. It shows respect, which I think is wonderful.

[5]__________, more in a week or two.

Bye for now,

Francesca

2 ANALYZE **Read the blog again and answer the questions.**

1 How long is Francesca going to live in Dar es Salaam?

____

2 What things does Francesca find very different in Tanzania?

____

____

3 Which thing(s) does she dislike? How do you know?

____

____

4 What is her favorite thing about Tanzania?

____

3 **Complete the blog with the phrases in the list.**

anyway | here's what | of course | so far | then

4 PLAN **Imagine you have gone to live in another country. How is it different from your home country? Use the ideas in the blog to help you. Make a plan.**

things you're already used to: ________________

things you don't like: ________________

things you like: ________________

the thing you like best: ________________

5 PRODUCE **Write a blog post (about 250 words) about your new country. Use your plan from Exercise 4. Make sure you include all the points in the checklist.**

✓ CHECKLIST

Explain which country you are in.

Say when you arrived and how long you are staying.

Give your general impression.

Say what you like best.

LISTENING

1 7.01 **Listen to three conversations. Circle the correct options.**

1 Sean *accepts* / *refuses* the invitation.
2 Eva *accepts* / *refuses* the invitation.
3 Bartie *accepts* / *refuses* the invitation.

2 7.01 **Listen again and mark the sentences T (true) or F (false). Then correct the false sentences.**

1
a Sean is always busy on the weekend. ☐
b He isn't interested in movies. ☐
c He accepts the invitation immediately. ☐

2
a Lucas invites Eva to a sports competition. ☐
b Eva agrees to ask some of her friends to come, too. ☐
c Lucas gives Eva some advice about what to bring. ☐

3
a Bartie declines the invitation because he'll be away. ☐
b Helena suggests something else they can do. ☐
c Helena decides to change her plans for this evening. ☐

3 7.01 **Listen again. Complete these parts of the dialogues.**

1
Nadia Well, listen, some of us are going to the movies on Saturday. Why [1] ________________ with us?
Sean No, wait, just a minute. I've changed my mind. [2] ________________ come. What time on Saturday?
Nadia I'm not sure yet, but it'll be in the evening. [3] ________________ me a call later, after I've talked to the others?

2
Lucas OK then. [4] ________________?
Eva [5] ________________ – I'd love to. I love walking. Thanks, Lucas.
Lucas No problem. [6] ________________ some friends with you?
Eva OK, I'll call some people.

3
Helena We're thinking of going to the town festival tonight. There's a barbecue and live music in the park. Why [7] ________________?
Bartie I'd love to, but you'll have to [8] ________________ this time.

PRONUNCIATION
Intonation – inviting, accepting, and refusing invitations Go to page 120.

DIALOGUE

4 **Put the dialogues in order.**

1
☐ A Well, how about coming with me to that new youth club in town?
☐ A Are you busy on Friday?
☐ A OK, let's meet there at seven.
☐ B Fine. I'll see you there.
☐ B That'd be great. I'd love to!
☐ B No, I'm not. Why?

2
☐ C Why don't you join us and bring someone?
☐ C Would you like to go to a party tonight?
☐ C A friend of mine, Jake. It's his birthday.
☐ D No, that's OK. I'd rather just go with you.
☐ D Whose party is it?
☐ D Yes, of course, thank you! I like parties.

PHRASES FOR FLUENCY

→ SB p.72

5 **Put the words in order to make phrases.**

0 point / good ____*good point*____
1 it / mention / don't ________________
2 it / rest / give / a ________________
3 yeah / well ________________
4 me / don't / wrong / get ________________
5 this / with / I'm / one / you / on ________________

6 **Complete the dialogues with phrases in Exercise 5.**

1 A It's great that you're helping me. Thanks a lot.
B Oh, ________________. It's a pleasure.

2 A Come on, let's go out for a walk.
B But the game is on TV in 15 minutes.
A Hmmm, ________________. Maybe we'll leave the walk until later.

3 A No, sorry – this music is really awful!
B ________________, Tess. Let's listen to something else.

4 A So you didn't like the present I gave you?
B Oh, no. ________________, I liked it. It's just that red isn't my favorite color.

5 A Mom, Angie won't give me my soccer ball back. Please tell her to.
B Oh, Rob, ________________, please! I have a really bad headache.

6 A So, why can't you come out tonight? Homework?
B ________________. French, English, and history!

READING AND USE OF ENGLISH
Word formation

EXAM GUIDE

This tests your vocabulary, grammar and spelling. You have to complete a text with eight gaps. The base word is given at the end of the line and you have to transform it so that it fits into the sentence.

- First, read the text through for general meaning.
- Remember that the word you have to use is at the end of the line with the gap.
- You have to transform the base word into an adjective, noun or adverb of the same word family. For example, you may have to add a negative prefix and/or transform the word type using a suffix.
- Re-read the sentence containing the new word to make sure it makes sense.
- Check if nouns need to be singular or plural.
- Spelling is important. It must be correct.

1 **For questions 1–8, read the text below. Use the word given in capitals at the end of some of the lines to form a word that fits in the gap in the same line. There is an example at the beginning (0).**

A Trip of a Lifetime!

I'm not usually a very 0 *adventurous* kind of person. I don't like having too much — ADVENTURE
1 ___________ in my life, but the trip that I took on the river at the Iguaçu Falls — EXCITE
between Brazil and Argentina was just fantastic and 2 ___________ unforgettable! — TOTAL
When you get close to the waterfalls, you get very wet from the spray. 3 ___________ , — FORTUNE
the day we went, it was cloudy, but we took some great photographs anyway.
The 4 ___________ was spectacular. — SCENE
Then we decided to go on a river trip to the falls. We got into an inflatable boat and sailed
up the river to the base of the waterfalls. The noise of the water was 5 ___________ — BELIEVE
loud! We had to be very 6 ___________ and hold on tight because the water was rough. — CARE
A couple of times we were worried for our 7 ___________ ! — SAFE
When we returned to dry land, we all agreed it had been a memorable – but at times
8 ___________ – trip! — SCARE

2 **For questions 1–8, read the text below. Use the word given in capitals at the end of some of the lines to form a word that fits in the gap in the same line. There is an example at the beginning (0).**

Sea View Bed and Breakfast – a review

We stayed here last month for three nights and had an 0 *enjoyable* stay overall. — ENJOY
We really liked the location – it's in the town centre, so restaurants and shops are nearby.
There are very 1 ___________ views over the beach. Breakfast was good and healthy — ATTRACT
as it included a 2 ___________ of fresh fruit. Also, the staff could not have been more — SELECT
attentive and 3 ___________ . — FRIEND
The bedroom was large and 4 ___________ , and so was the bathroom. So, what was — SPACE
the problem?
We had three almost 5 ___________ nights. The bed was the hardest and most — SLEEP
6 ___________ bed I have ever tried to sleep in! The noise from the street outside — COMFORT
the window meant it was absolutely 7 ___________ to get a good night's rest. — POSSIBLE
So, it's 8 ___________ that we would go back. It's a shame because Sea View has — DOUBT
so many good things going for it.

8 CRIME AND PUNISHMENT

Grammar rap!

GRAMMAR

Reported speech (review)

→ SB p.76

1 ★★☆ **Report what the burglar said to a police officer. Complete the sentences using reported speech.**

0 "I broke into an apartment yesterday."
He said *he had broken into an apartment the day* before.

1 "I stole a laptop and some jewelry."
He said ______________________ a laptop and some jewelry.

2 "I feel really terrible about stealing someone's things."
He said ______________________ really terrible about stealing someone's things.

3 "I am going to say sorry to them."
He said ______________________ sorry to them.

4 "I will never commit a crime again."
He said ______________________ a crime again.

2 ★★☆ **Rewrite these sentences using reported speech.**

1 "I'm really upset," said Mr. Jones after the break-in.
____

2 "The burglar broke into the house through the bathroom window," a neighbor told the police.
____

3 "This is the first time I've been caught shoplifting," the boy told the store manager.
____

4 "We were waiting on the subway platform when it happened," said the students.
____

5 "Pickpockets in London can make £4,000 a week by stealing wallets, smartphones, and laptops," a police officer told us.
____

6 "I will think about putting security cameras in the store," the store owner said after the robbery.
____

7 "My son is going to report the mugging to the police," said Mrs. Roberts.
____

3 ★★☆ **Rewrite what the people said in direct speech.**

0 The residents asked the police if they had arrested the mugger yet.
Have you arrested the mugger yet?

1 The security guard told the police that he had seen the shoplifter run across the parking lot.
____
____

2 The thief told the police officer that he had never been arrested before.
____
____

3 The police officer asked a neighbor if anybody was living in the house next door.
____
____

4 The lawyer told the gang that they would probably be sentenced to three years in prison.
____
____

5 The woman said that she was going to report the scam to the police.
____
____

Reported questions, requests, and imperatives

→ SB p.77

4 ★☆☆ **Circle the correct options.**

1 "Sit down."
The police officer told me *sit down* / *to sit down*.

2 "Write your statement on the form."
She told me *write* / *to write* my statement on the form.

3 "Don't worry."
She told me *not to worry* / *don't worry*.

4 "Did you see the thief?"
She asked me if I *had seen* / *saw* the thief.

5 "Do you live in this building?"
She asked me whether I *lived* / *had lived* in this building.

6 "Are you going to interview anyone else?"
I asked her if she *had interviewed* / *was going to interview* anyone else.

5 ★★☆ Complete the sentences.

1 "Write down your name and address."
He asked me ______________________

2 "Stand up."
She told us ______________________

3 "Do you know the victim?"
He asked us ______________________

4 "Describe the mugger."
He asked me ______________________

5 "Fill out the form."
She told him ______________________

6 "Have you been robbed before?"
He asked her ______________________

6 ★★☆ Match the sentences (1–8) with the sentence beginnings (a–h). Then complete the sentences.

1 "No, I won't tell you where we've hidden the phones," said the boy. ☐
2 "Where did you hide the phones?" asked the police officer. ☐
3 "No, I was in the car when they hid the phones," said the boy. ☐
4 "Come to the police station and make a statement," said the police officer. ☐
5 "You must tell me who the other two boys are," said the police officer. ☐
6 "Alright. I'll come to the police station with you," said the boy. ☐
7 "Can I call my mom?" asked the boy. ☐
8 "Do you have a phone?" asked the police officer. ☐

a The boy asked if ______________________
b The police officer told the boy ______________________
c The police officer demanded to know ______________________
d The boy refused to tell the police ______________________
e The police officer asked the boy where ______________________
f The police officer asked the boy if ______________________
g The boy explained that ______________________
h The boy agreed ______________________

7 ★★★ Read the script for a play. Then report the dialogue.

Mark is waiting for the bus when a guy walks up to him.

Mugger Do you want to survive tonight?
Mark I don't understand what you mean.
Mugger The night can have a good ending or a bad ending. It's up to you.
Mark Please tell me what you mean by that. Are you a mugger? I only have $20.
Mugger That's fine.

[Mark gives him the money. The mugger moves closer. Mark is scared.]

Mark Are you going to hurt me?
Mugger Thanks, buddy.

[hugs the boy and walks off]

Mark was surprised – he couldn't believe that the mugger had hugged him!

He asked me [1] ______________________
I told him I [2] ______________________
He said that the night [3] ______________________
I asked him [4] ______________________
I wanted to know [5] ______________________
I told him that [6] ______________________
He said that [7] ______________________
I asked him [8] ______________________

GET IT RIGHT!

Reported questions

In reported questions, we don't use question word order, but statement word order.

✓ *I'll ask where I can find the station.*
✗ *I'll ask where ~~can I~~ find the station.*

We don't need the auxiliary *do*.

✓ *They asked when it started.*
✗ *They asked when ~~did it start~~.*

If it is a yes / no question, we need to include *if*.

✓ *I'll ask if he has arrived yet.*
✗ *I'll ~~ask he~~ has arrived yet.*

Correct the sentences.

1 He asked how much did I pay for the phone.
____
2 Everyone asked when did the article have to be finished.
____
3 I asked my mom I could go out.
____
4 I asked my parents which school will I go to when we move.
____

VOCABULARY

Crime

SB p.76

1 ★☆☆ **Complete the sentences with the correct word or phrase from the list.**

arrested | breaking in | committing a crime | fine | got caught | got into trouble | murder | murderers | prison | prisoner

1 Some criminals must pay a [1] ________________ instead of going to [2] ________________ .

2 An escaped [3] ________________ was [4] ________________ again this morning as he was [5] ________________ . He [6] ________________ while he was stealing a car.

3 A man almost [7] ________________ with the police when they saw him climbing into a house through the window. They thought he was [8] ________________ , but he'd just forgotten his key.

4 [9] ________________ is a very serious crime and [10] ________________ are often sent to prison for life.

2 ★★☆ **Put the pictures about the story of Bob the burglar in order. Then write the story with some of the words and phrases in Exercise 1.**

A ☐

____

____

____

____

B ☐

____

____

____

____

C ☐

____

____

____

____

D ☐

____

____

____

____

3 ★★☆ **Read the clues and complete the puzzle.**

1 a building where criminals are kept as a punishment
2 a person who kills another person
3 to enter a building illegally with the intention of stealing
4 money that has to be paid for breaking a rule or law
5 a person who has been put in prison
6 The mugger got ____________ by the police and taken away.
7 If you ____________ a crime, you will be punished.
8 the crime of killing another person
9 The robbers broke ____________ the bank through a tunnel.
10 The police ____________ a person when they know or think they have broken the law.

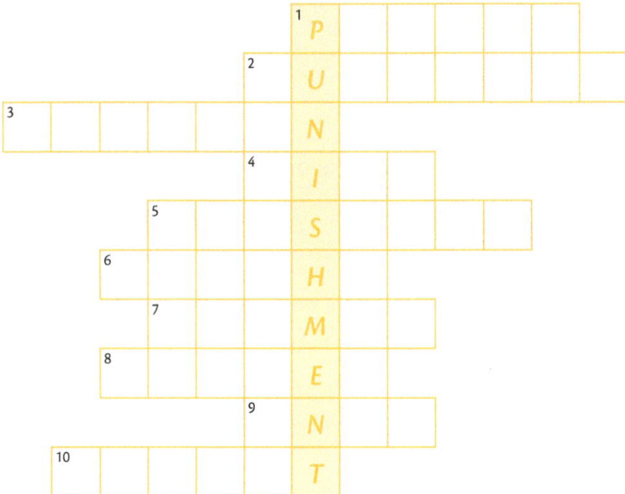

Reporting verbs

SB p.79

4 ★★☆ **Circle the correct words.**

1 "I won't go to the police station."
The boy *refused* / *agreed* to go to the police station.

2 "I was in the yard when it happened."
The woman *refused* / *explained* that she had been in the yard when it happened.

3 "Yes, you're right. It's my fault."
The girl *agreed* / *recommended* that it was her fault.

4 "I need you to tell me what happened."
The man *told* / *demanded* to know what had happened.

5 "I was with my friends at a club at 9 p.m. last night."
The man *claimed* / *agreed* that he had been with his friends at a club at 9 p.m. that night.

6 "Empty your pockets for me, please."
The police officer *explained* / *told* him to empty his pockets.

7 "We're going to the park. Would you like to come with us?"
They *persuaded* / *invited* me to go to the park with them.

8 "If you like pizza, then Pizza Shed on Main Street is the place to go."
She *recommended* / *invited* having pizza at Pizza Shed.

9 "I know it's hard, but I think you should try to learn Japanese."
He *invited* / *encouraged* me to learn Japanese.

10 "OK, OK, I'll go to the concert with you."
I *persuaded* / *agreed* her to go to the concert with me.

REFERENCE

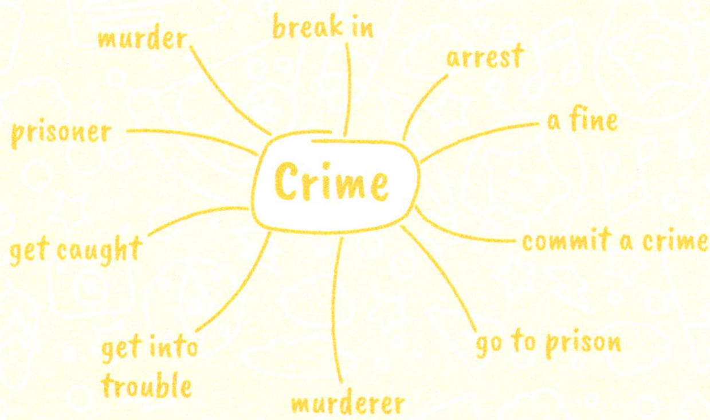

VOCABULARY *EXTRA*

1 **Complete the table with the verbs in the list.**

~~arrest~~ | mug | ~~murder~~ | punish
scam | shoplift | steal | suspect

Crime verbs	Other verbs
murder	*arrest*

2 **Match the verbs (1–6) with the phrases (a–f).**

1 to mug ☐
2 to scam ☐
3 to punish ☐
4 to shoplift ☐
5 to steal ☐
6 to suspect ☐

a a video game from a store
b a tourist out of some money
c a car from outside a house
d a criminal for a crime
e a person in the street
f someone of a crime

3 **Choose one of the groups of words and write a short story using them.**

A

arrest | scam | steal

B

get into trouble | shoplift | suspect

A life of crime ...
IN THE ANIMAL KINGDOM

We love animals, especially our pets, but did you know that these cute creatures sometimes break the law?

Most cats catch birds and mice, then bring them home for their owners, but not Oscar the tabby cat. He steals from neighbors' yards. Every day he arrives home with socks and underwear from clothes lines, gardening gloves, toys, and other small items. Oscar's owners don't know what to do. How do you stop a cat's criminal activities? They can't return the stolen goods because there are too many of them, and they don't know who they belong to. Instead, they've asked local residents to report missing items to them. They then invite the victims of Oscar's crimes to identify their belongings from among his collection.

Oscar's not the only cat with criminal habits. There's Birgit the cat in New Zealand, who specializes in stealing men's socks, and a cat named Sir-Whines-A-Lot in the US, who steals money. He's an office cat and when customers are paying, he waits for an opportunity to take some money. He got caught when an employee discovered a small pile of cash on the floor one morning. When the office explained what was happening on social media and that they'd given Sir-Whines-A-Lot's illegal earnings to charity, they received more contributions from their customers!

Anyone who's tried eating sandwiches on the beach will know that seagulls don't just eat fish. Seagulls are bigger than you'd think and can become aggressive when they're trying to get your tasty snack. There's a seagull in Scotland that doesn't just steal food, but shoplifts, too! This criminal bird regularly hangs out outside a bakery. He waits until there aren't any customers in the store, then walks in, helps himself to a bag of chips, and carries it outside to eat. The owners are so used to it that they don't say anything any more and the shoplifting seagull has become a local celebrity.

People say that the octopus is an intelligent animal, but Otto, who lives in an aquarium in Germany, has a criminal mind. He uses his intelligence to cause chaos. He regularly commits small crimes such as throwing rocks at the glass wall of his tank, but his most serious crime so far was to cause an electricity blackout at the aquarium on three nights in a row. Despite their investigations, the staff couldn't find the cause of the blackout. They agreed that the only solution was to spend the night in the aquarium and watch. That's how Otto got caught. When he climbed to the top of his tank and shot water at the light above it, the electricity was automatically shut off for safety.

Then there's the crow in Canada who disrupted a crime-scene investigation by flying away with a knife. The police reported that an officer had chased the bird until it dropped the knife!

And finally, there's Jack the husky in the US who has been banned from entering the state of Maryland, but nobody knows why!

READING

1 **Read the article and check (✓) the crimes mentioned.**

burglary ☐ | murder ☐ | pickpocketing ☐
shoplifting ☐ | theft ☐ | vandalism ☐

2 **Complete the sentences with the names of one or more of the animals in the article.**

1 ________________ interrupted police work.
2 ________________ has/have committed an unknown crime.
3 ________________ is/are guilty of theft.
4 ________________ has/have broken the law in several different ways.
5 ________________ got caught while breaking the law.
6 ________________'s crime had a positive result in the end.

3 CRITICAL THINKING **Read the article again and <u>underline</u> the sentences that contain extra information that is not absolutely necessary to understand the text.**

4 **Choose one of the animals in the article and write a short story written from their perspective.**

An essay

1 INPUT Read the essay quickly. What is it about? Circle the best answer.

A How crime makes people rich
B The reasons people become criminals
C The best way to prevent crime

POVERTY IS THE CAUSE OF CRIME

1 Crime is a serious problem in every country around the world. Some people think that one of the main causes of crime is poverty. Other people have claimed that poverty does not have a direct link to crime.

2 [a] ________________ , there are many reasons why people commit crimes and poverty is one of them. For example, a teenager who has no money, but wants the same sneakers as his or her classmates, goes out and shoplifts them.

3 [b] ________________ , it isn't just poor people who commit crimes. Wealthy people with good jobs, nice homes, and loving families also break the law. However, they generally commit different types of crimes for a variety of reasons. [c] ________________ , they may be risk-takers and enjoy the thrill. [d] ________________ , children from a poor family with a very caring mother and father are unlikely to commit a crime. They have love and security, and they're happy.

4 [e] ________________ , the main reason for teenagers and young adults committing crimes is a lack of support from their families and people around them. They often feel unloved and they have few good role models.

5 [f] ________________ , poverty is undoubtedly a cause of crime, but it is not the only one. Governments need to improve living standards for all their citizens and we must all try to give more support to children and teenagers in need.

2 Complete the essay with the phrases in the list.

first | for example | however | in my opinion
on the other hand | to conclude

3 ANALYZE Read the essay again and match the headings with paragraphs 1–5.

Argument for ☐
The conclusion ☐
The writer's opinion ☐
Argument against ☐
Introduction presenting the issue ☐

4 PLAN Think about the advantages and disadvantages of stricter punishments for criminals. Add two advantages and two disadvantages to each column.

Advantages	Disadvantages
It will discourage criminals from committing other crimes.	*Sending someone to prison, where they mix with other criminals, will do more harm than good.*
________________	________________
________________	________________
________________	________________
________________	________________
________________	

5 Write a plan for the other paragraphs of the essay.

- Introduction
- Your opinion
- Conclusion

6 PRODUCE Write an essay with the title "Stricter punishments will reduce crime" (250 words). Use your plan from Exercises 4 and 5. Make sure you follow all the points in the checklist.

CHECKLIST

Use formal language.
Use the linking phrases in Exercise 2 to connect sentences and paragraphs.
Try to use vocabulary from the unit.

LISTENING

1 8.01 **Listen to the dialogue. Mark the sentences T (true) or F (false).**

1 A note came in the mail the other day for Jane. ☐
2 The note told Jane to pick up a package from the post office. ☐
3 They wanted Jane to pay an extra $50. ☐
4 Jane never received the package. ☐
5 Jane's friend doesn't think it was a large amount of money. ☐
6 The police told her that hundreds of people had been tricked by the scam. ☐

2 8.01 **Listen again. Complete these parts of the dialogue.**

1
A You'll never guess what I've done.
B Uh oh, Jane, ________________ !
A I've been really stupid.

2
A Yes, I paid it online. There was a website and I paid immediately.
B Really? Were ________________ a package?

3
B ________________ ? Was the package delivered?
A No, it was a scam.
B ________________ !
A There was ________________ in the local newspaper the other day.

4
B Have you reported it to the police?
A Yes, I have. They told me that hundreds of people have been tricked.
B ________________ !

3 8.02 **Listen to the dialogue between Kate and a police officer. Then answer the questions.**

1 Who stole Kate's bag?
____
2 What did Kate say the girl looked like?
____
3 Where was Kate's bag when it was stolen?
____
4 What did the police officer advise Kate not to do?
____
5 Why did the police officer tell Kate she should be careful with her bag?
____
6 What did Kate say was in her bag?
____

DIALOGUE

4 **Complete the dialogues with the phrases in the list.**

Tell me | No way | You'll never guess what
Really | There was a story
You won't believe what happened to
That's awful | I heard a really sad story | What

1
A ________________________ happened to me!
B ________________________ ?
A I've won a short story writing competition.
B That's amazing. Well done.

2
C ________________________ yesterday.
D ________________________ .
C Mrs. Price's cat disappeared last week and now Mrs. Price is really lonely.
D ________________________ !

3
E ________________________ me last night.
F What?
E I fell asleep on the train and I didn't wake up until it got to San Francisco.
F ________________________ ! That's a long way from Denver.

4
G ________________________ in the paper the other day about our art teacher.
H ________________________ ?
G Yes, apparently, his grandfather was a famous artist. There's an exhibition of his paintings at the art gallery next week.

5 **Write a short account of a time when you or someone you know had something stolen or was pickpocketed. Where were you/they? Who took it? What did they take?**

PRONUNCIATION
Intonation – expressing surprise
Go to page 120.

WRITING
An informal email or letter

EXAM GUIDE

Among the four questions to choose from, there is often an informal email or a letter. Your answer should be 140–190 words long.

- Always write a brief plan before you start writing.
- Remember to start and close your email/letter correctly.
- Include all the information requested in the question.
- Choose an appropriate writing style for the person you are writing to.
- Keep within the word limit and remember you have about 40 minutes for each part of the Writing test.

1 **Read the exam task. Underline the important information.**

You have received an email from your English-speaking friend.

I've just heard that your bike's been stolen and I'm a bit concerned for you. When and where did it happen? How did you feel? How did you manage to get home? Did you report it to the police? Please let me know all the details.
See you soon,
Peter

Write your email in 140–190 words.

2 **Read Anya's answer to the task. Which part of the question has she forgotten to answer?**

Anya

Great to hear from you, and thanks for your concern. Of course, I was very puzzled when I got to the bike rack and couldn't find my bike. Then I felt angry with the thief. How was I going to get home? I didn't have any money on me and it would take me ages to walk. Luckily, I always have my phone with me, so I rang my mum and explained to her what had happened. She told me to wait there and she'd come and pick me up. She said we could go together and report it to the headteacher.

It's annoying because three other people have had their bikes stolen, too, and that's just in the last week! I really hope the school will do something about it.

Oh – I'm sorry I have to go now. The police are here. The headteacher called them. I'll send you a message later to let you know what they say.

Bye,
Anya

3 **Look at the questions Anya asked herself before writing. Read the email again to find the answers.**

1 How did I feel when I first realised the bike was missing?

______

2 Then, when I realised it had been stolen, how did I feel?

______

3 How else could I get home?

______

4 Who could come to help me?

______

5 Who should I report the theft to?

______

4 **Read the task and write your answer in 140–190 words.**

You have received an email from your English-speaking friend.

I'm so sorry to hear that you've been mugged. That's really awful! When and where did it happen? Were you hurt in the attack? How do you feel now? What did the mugger take? Did you report it to the police?
Best,
Theo

Write your email in 140–190 words.

5 **Ask a friend to read your story and complete the sentences about it.**

I thought ______ was good.

I *thought / didn't think* the email explained everything.

You could improve it by ______

______

______

The language used was ______

______

CONSOLIDATION

LISTENING

1 🔊 8.05 **Listen and circle the correct option (A, B, or C).**

1 How many times has the boy's bike been stolen?
   A twice in two years
   B three times in two years
   C twice in three years

2 Where was the bike stolen from?
   A a park
   B outside a parking garage
   C near some stores

3 Why is the boy going to the police station now?
   A to give a description of his bike
   B to help the police find it
   C to identify a bike they've found

2 🔊 8.05 **Listen again. Complete each sentence with between two and four words.**

1 The boy got the money to buy his bike by cutting ______________ cars.
2 The boy had ______________ on it but the thieves cut it off.
3 His bike was stolen in ______________ .
4 The boy doesn't think the police are ______________ his bike.
5 The police have ______________ station that fits the description.

GRAMMAR

3 **Circle the correct options.**

1 George told me *to leave* / *leave* right away.
2 We aren't *allow* / *allowed* to go into the lab without permission.
3 I don't think I'll ever get used to *drive* / *driving* on the left.
4 Does your school *make* / *let* you wear anything you want?
5 A lot of people don't like the weather here, but they soon *are* / *get* used to it.
6 I never want to get up at six o'clock, but my parents *let* / *make* me.
7 The new student asked me where *I was from* / *was I from*.
8 The teacher encouraged us to *take* / *taking* the exam.
9 I invited Lily *to come* / *come* with us.
10 Tina asked us what *did we have* / *we had* to do.

4 **Complete the sentences using the correct form of the word in parentheses.**

0 My dad says I have to get up at 7:00. (make)
   My dad makes me get up at 7:00.
1 Our teacher says it's OK to use a dictionary. (let)
   Our teacher ______________ .
2 We can't go into that room. (allowed)
   We ______________ .
3 The principal told us to clean the playground. (make)
   The principal ______________ .
4 Last week, our mom said we couldn't watch TV. (let)
   Our mom ______________ .

VOCABULARY

5 **Complete the phrasal verbs.**

1 Yesterday I just hung __________ with my friends.
2 Could you look __________ my cat while I'm away on the weekend?
3 What time does the plane take __________ ?
4 Grandpa decided to take __________ playing the piano when he was 60.
5 My sister and I have always gotten __________ well together.
6 We didn't want to stop, so we just carried __________ walking.
7 I waited for hours, but Maxine didn't show __________ .
8 My mom gave __________ eating meat years ago.

6 **Complete each sentence with one word.**

1 If you break that window, you'll get into __________ with the neighbors.
2 I don't mind what we listen to. It's all the __________ to me.
3 Anna had to pay a __________ because she parked in the wrong place.
4 I don't know anyone who has ever __________ a crime.
5 She stole some money and went to __________ for three months.
6 There was a __________-in at the supermarket. The thieves stole a lot of food and money.
7 The thief was __________ while he was cutting through the bike lock.
8 Hey, stop asking me that question! __________ and for all, I don't know!
9 Harry always says "please" and "thank you." He's so __________ .
10 Camilla only thinks about herself. She's really __________ .

DIALOGUE

7 8.06 **Complete the conversation with the phrases in the list. Then listen and check.**

be honest | don't mention it
I know how you feel | get me wrong
I'm with you | in fact | point | yeah, I

Tessa Here's your GPS back. Thanks a lot for lending it to me.

Jack [1]________________ . I hope it was useful.

Tessa Yes, it was, thanks. But listen, Jack – don't [2]________________ , but maybe you should get a new one.

Jack Why? Is it out of date?

Tessa Well, [3]________________ mean, it was useful, like I said. But three times it tried to make us drive the wrong way down a one-way street. I guess they changed the directions, but the GPS didn't know that.

Jack So, [4]________________ , I don't need a new GPS – I just need to update the map.

Tessa Well, to [5]________________ , that's not the only problem. The display is a little old-fashioned, too.

Jack Yeah, good [6]________________ . And the battery isn't very good either, is it?

Tessa No. So really it all adds up to just one thing – buy a new one!

Jack Yeah, [7]________________ on that. I just don't have any money right now so it's going to have to wait.

Tessa Yes, [8]________________ . I spent all my money over the weekend. Well, see you!

READING

8 **Read the stories and answer the questions.**

THE WORLD'S WORST CRIMINALS?

1 Recently, police in Calgary, Canada got a call from a woman who said that her home had been broken into. Jewelry was missing, all the home electronics, such as the TV, laptops, and tablets, were gone, windows had been smashed, and so on. It wasn't surprising that the woman was crying when the police officer arrived. The officer was 37-year-old Charanjit Meharu, who is of Indian origin. While Officer Meharu was checking the crime scene, the woman's phone rang. It was her father, and she began to tell her father – speaking in French – that it wasn't a real burglary: she and her boyfriend had hidden the things, broken the window, and made up the whole story in order to get money from the insurance company. What the woman didn't know is that Officer Meharu speaks seven languages: English, Punjabi, Hindi, Urdu, Arabic, Gujarati – and French!

2 A few weeks ago a teenager was walking the streets looking for a bike. He found one parked outside a building. There was no one nearby, so he started cutting through the bike lock. He was just about to ride away when a police officer suddenly appeared. The boy hadn't noticed that the building was, in fact, a police station – and that there was a security camera on the wall above the bike! The officer had watched what the boy was doing on the screen inside the building, but had let him finish the job first. When he asked him what he was doing, the boy thought for a second, then replied that he was just taking the bike away. He pointed to a sign on the wall that said cyclists weren't allowed to park their bikes there! The police officer smiled but arrested the boy all the same!

STORY 1

1 Why was the woman crying when the police officer arrived?

____

2 What had the woman and her boyfriend done? Why?

____

3 How did Officer Meharu know that the burglary was not real?

____

STORY 2

4 What didn't the boy realize?

____

5 When did the police officer go out to speak to the boy?

____

6 Why did the police officer smile?

____

WRITING

9 **Find another example of a criminal making a stupid mistake and write the story. Write about 150–200 words.**

9 IT'S A MYSTERY!

Grammar rap!

GRAMMAR

Modals of deduction (present)

→ SB p.86

1 ★☆☆ **Circle the correct options.**

1 They could be Colombian because they're speaking *Spanish / German*.
2 It can't be a spider; it only has *six / eight* legs.
3 Otis must really love that movie. He's seen it *once / ten times*.
4 There can't be anyone at home. All the lights are *on / off*.
5 Jess must travel a lot. Her passport's full of *visa stamps / blank pages*.
6 Bella might be tired. She's been *working hard / doing nothing* all day.
7 They might not speak English. They're *French / American*.
8 Declan must like heavy metal. He *always / never* listens to anything else!

2 ★★☆ **Complete the dialogue with *must / can't / might*.**

Rachel Look, Claudia Woods is on Facebook. I'm going to send her a friend request. There – done.
Isaac Wow, she has five hundred friends. She [1]__________ be really popular.
Rachel Well, they [2]__________ all be real friends. No one can have that many. Not even Claudia.
Isaac That's true. She [3]__________ not really know most of them.
Rachel Yes, 20 proper friends at the most. The rest of them [4]__________ just be friends of friends. She probably just accepts anyone who wants to be her friend.
Isaac Why does she do that?
Rachel I don't know. She [5]__________ be a bit lonely. Maybe it makes her feel better.
Isaac But that [6]__________ work. Having a lot of false friends doesn't make anyone feel better.
Rachel Oh look. She [7]__________ be online because she's replied to my request already.
Isaac And what does she say?
Rachel I [8]__________ believe it. She said no!

should(n't) have

→ SB p.87

3 ★☆☆ **Complete the sentences with phrases in the list.**

should invite | shouldn't have gone
should have invited | should have watched
shouldn't go | shouldn't have said
shouldn't say | should watch

1 The documentary last night was really good. You __________ it.
2 That old house looks really dangerous. My mom says we __________ inside.
3 You __________ Joe. He'll be upset if you don't.
4 Maxwell __________ anything. It was our secret!
5 We __________ things if we don't really mean them.
6 There's a great movie on TV tonight. You __________ it.
7 The party was really boring. We __________.
8 You __________ Kayla to your party. She was really upset that you didn't.

4 ★★☆ **Read the story and complete the sentences with *should(n't) have* and a verb in the list.**

charge | go | leave | ~~take~~ | tell | wear

Georgina went on a bike ride. After about 10 km, she had a problem with her bike, but she couldn't fix it because she had no tools with her. She took out her phone, but she couldn't make a call because her phone battery was dead. She decided to get a bus home, but when she looked for her wallet, it wasn't in her pocket. There was nothing she could do but walk. It started raining and she got really wet because she didn't have a jacket. Two hours later, when she finally got home, her mom was really angry with her because she had been worried about her. It's the last time Georgina is going on a bike ride without planning it properly.

0 She *should have taken* some tools with her.
1 She __________ her phone before leaving.
2 She __________ her wallet at home.
3 She __________ a jacket.
4 She __________ her mom where she was going.
5 She __________ on a bike ride without planning it properly!

5 ★★★ **Complete the conversations with your own ideas. Use *should(n't) have*.**

0 A I'm so tired today.
You should have gone to bed earlier.

1 A This T-shirt is too small for me.
B ______

2 A Jake's really angry with me.
B ______

3 A I'm so thirsty, but I don't have anything to drink.
B ______

4 A I don't have enough money left to take the bus.
B ______

5 A I don't understand this homework at all.
B ______

Modals of deduction (past)

→ SB p.89

6 ★☆☆ **Match the sentences.**

1 Peter crashed Nicola's scooter again. ☐
2 Liam ate everything. ☐
3 But he was too polite to ask for some food. ☐
4 Rosa's soccer team won the championship. ☐
5 Andy didn't eat anything. ☐
6 But it's always difficult to know what she's feeling. ☐

a She must have been happy.
b She can't have been happy.
c Nadia might have been happy.
d He must have been hungry.
e He can't have been hungry.
f He could have been hungry.

7 ★★☆ **Complete the text with the verbs in parentheses and the correct modal verbs.**

Police are still looking for the multi-millionaire banker Cecil Montgomery who disappeared from his home last week. At first, they were sure criminals [1]______ (take) him from the family home, but now they are investigating the possibility that he [2]______ (disappear) on purpose. It seems that he was having financial problems and owed a lot of people a lot of money and police believe that he [3]______ (go) into hiding to escape from these people. One thing we know for sure is that he [4]______ (leave) the country as police found his passport in his office desk. Police are now asking members of the public for their help. They feel certain that someone [5]______ (see) Cecil in the last few days and they are asking that person to come forward and help them with their investigation.

8 ★★★ **Complete the sentences with your own ideas. Use modals of deduction.**

1 Our principal looks really happy. She ______
______
2 I recognize his face. I'm sure ______
______
3 Nobody went to their party. They ______
______
4 I'm not sure how I fell off my bike. I ______
______
5 Our cat is missing. I'm worried ______
______
6 Josie is two hours late – ______
______
7 The baby fell asleep in two minutes – ______
______
8 Perry doesn't have any money – ______
______

GET IT RIGHT!

Modals of deduction: past

Learners sometimes use *can have* for speculating about past events when *could have* is needed. But remember, we use *can't have* in the negative.

✓ *He could have known the truth.*
✗ *He ~~can have~~ known the truth.*
✓ *He can't have known the truth.*

Choose the correct sentence in each pair.

1 a It must be in the garage. It can have been put anywhere else.
b It must be in the garage. It can't have been put anywhere else.

2 a Do you think it could have been someone else?
b Do you think it can have been someone else?

3 a She can't have known about it because nobody told her.
b She could have known about it because nobody told her.

4 a I don't think we can have managed it without your help.
b I don't think we could have managed it without your help.

5 a They can't have gotten there in time. Their car was too slow.
b They could have gotten there in time. Their car was too slow.

VOCABULARY

Mysteries

→ SB p.86

1 ★☆☆ **Find eight words about mysteries in the wordsearch.**

N	T	E	R	O	F	E	A	K	R	I	O	W	S	M	O
K	B	P	U	Z	Z	L	I	N	G	A	W	U	U	J	T
N	O	X	H	P	S	H	Z	Z	V	Q	U	E	O	G	R
E	X	T	R	A	T	E	R	R	E	S	T	R	I	A	L
I	H	E	A	N	R	P	A	R	I	E	O	Y	R	E	R
L	A	I	A	N	A	O	D	D	A	C	B	D	E	A	N
A	I	L	V	O	N	T	R	M	O	R	U	I	T	E	S
W	K	N	A	R	G	F	E	W	D	E	X	W	S	R	Y
T	L	E	A	T	E	A	S	P	C	T	B	E	Y	H	F
S	E	U	N	E	X	P	L	A	I	N	E	D	M	T	Y

1 ________________
2 ________________
3 ________________
4 ________________
5 ________________
6 ________________
7 ________________
8 ________________

2 ★★☆ **Circle the correct words.**

1 Hannah hasn't returned my call, which is really *strange* / *unexplained*.
2 I didn't really understand the end of the movie. It was a bit *secret* / *puzzling*.
3 Scientists believe the object is *odd* / *alien* and from another planet.
4 I don't want you to tell anyone. It's top *puzzling* / *secret*.
5 Paul's behavior is a bit *alien* / *mysterious*. I think he might have a secret!
6 I'm sure I had a $10 bill in my wallet, but it isn't here. That's *secret* / *odd*.
7 I didn't like that man. He was very *extraterrestrial* / *strange*.
8 To this day, the disappearance of our neighbor is still *alien* / *unexplained*.

Expressions with *go*

→ SB p.89

3 ★☆☆ **Match the sentences or the parts of the sentences.**

1 I don't think the party's ☐
2 We've set the dates so now we need to go one step further and ☐
3 We had a great time at the concert. ☐
4 I think it goes without saying ☐
5 The movie was so slow and boring and ☐
6 That funny video clip ☐

a We all went crazy when they played our favorite song!
b it went on for hours.
c has gone viral!
d decide where to go!
e going very well.
f that you aren't coming in here.

4 ★★☆ **Complete the conversations with the expressions in the list.**

crazy | for | on | one step further
really well | up | viral | without saying

1 A How much are the movie tickets?
B $12. They've gone ________________ recently. They were $9.
2 A Your sister likes dancing, doesn't she?
B Likes?! She goes ________________ when she gets the chance to dance!
3 A How was the exam?
B It went ________________ . I think I've passed.
4 A Do you want to lift 100kg again?
B I think I'll go ________________ and try 110 kg.
5 A Why are you so late?
B Sorry. My music lesson went ________________ longer than usual.
6 A Did you watch that video clip I posted?
B Yes. It's amazing. It went ________________ immediately!
7 A Have you decided what to order?
B I think I'll go ________________ the vegetable curry, please.
8 A So are you going to invite me to your party?
B Of course – it goes ________________ . You are my best friend, after all.

REFERENCE

Mysteries

- unexplained mystery
- mysterious writing
- strange figure
- extraterrestrial spaceman
- secret code
- alien life form
- puzzling pictures
- odd behavior

Expressions with *go*

- go for (something)
- go one step further
- go ahead
- go well
- go up
- go without saying
- go crazy
- go viral

VOCABULARY *EXTRA*

1 **Match the words (1–7) with the definitions (a–g).**

1 astonished ☐
2 confused ☐
3 invisible ☐
4 frightened ☐
5 magic ☐
6 suspicious ☐
7 weird ☐

a scared
b having special powers
c feeling something is wrong
d very surprised
e strange or odd
f unable to understand
g impossible to see

2 **Complete the table with the words in Exercise 1.**

Words to describe people, things, or situations	Words to describe how people feel
______________	______________
______________	______________
______________	______________
______________	______________

3 **Circle the correct words.**

1 The text was so small that it was almost *weird / invisible*.
2 We were *astonished / frightened* when our project won the prize.
3 I didn't feel happy about going into the cave. In fact, I was *weird / frightened*.
4 The explanation wasn't clear and we were all *invisible / confused*.
5 Some of the paintings were unusual and others were totally *invisible / weird*.
6 The message didn't make sense and I began to feel *magic / suspicious* that something wasn't right.
7 It comes on automatically – it's like *astonished / magic*!

4 **Complete the sentences about your own experiences.**

1 I felt confused when ______________________________
____
2 I was astonished when ______________________________
____
3 I felt frightened when ______________________________
____
4 I was suspicious when ______________________________
____

SOLVING THE WORLD'S MYSTERIES WITH SCIENCE

THE NAZCA LINES OF PERU

The Nazca Lines in Peru are huge! They were drawn on the ground by digging shallow lines in the earth. The lines were made by removing the red stone that covers the surface so that the white rock below could be seen. An area of 492 square kilometers in the Nazca desert in southern Peru is covered with 800 straight lines, 300 geometric shapes, and 70 simple pictures, which include birds, spiders, fish, and sharks. Some of these pictures are nearly 200 meters wide and the longest lines reach up to 48 kilometers.

What's so mysterious about these lines? Well, although they date back to between the years 400 and 650, they were only discovered in the 1930s. The reason is that the lines and pictures are invisible from the ground and can only be seen from the air. It was only when airplanes started flying over the area that people realized that the lines were there. When they were first discovered, people were astonished and confused. Of course, this led to the question: how did these pictures get there all those years ago? Surely they couldn't have been made without modern tools. People didn't have the ability to fly so long ago. Or did they? Author Jim Woodman suggested that the Nazca people could have invented simple hot-air balloons and used them to produce the art. He even built a working balloon using the same materials they would have used. Not many people were convinced by his ideas though. Other people suggested the lines might be extraterrestrial and that they were the work of aliens visiting Earth. More and more theories were offered and one of the great modern mysteries was created.

However, when some wooden sticks were found in the ground in the area and carbon-dated, it showed that they were the same age as the drawings. This discovery made scientists wonder if the Nazca people might have put these sticks in the ground to help them do the drawings. By placing the sticks in the correct positions and connecting them with long ropes, the Nazca people could have used them to draw the lines to make the pictures. One scientist, Dr. Joe Nickell of the University of Kentucky, was so sure that this was the answer that he decided to try to show how it could be done. Using only the tools that the Nazca people might have had, he set about trying to draw a huge picture of a bird on a piece of land. With the help of several friends, it took him only a few hours to produce a perfect Nazca picture and to show at long last how these pictures probably got there.

Among the mysteries of the Nazca Lines, there is one clear fact. The lines and pictures can still be seen after around 1,500 years because of the climate. They are in a desert with very little wind and less than 2.5 cm of rain a year. This explains why the lines are in such good condition today.

READING

1 **Read the article and choose the correct option.**

The Nazca Lines were made …

A over a thousand years ago.

B nearly 100 years ago.

C recently.

2 **Read the article again and answer the questions.**

1 How were the lines drawn?

____

2 What invention led to the discovery of the Nazca Lines? Why?

____

3 What did Jim Woodman make?

____

4 What discovery gave Dr. Joe Nickell the idea for his theory?

____

5 Why can we still see the Nazca Lines today?

____

3 CRITICAL THINKING **Find evidence in the text that supports the theories about the Nazca Lines.**

1 The Nazca people could fly.

____

2 The Nazca Lines were made by aliens.

____

3 The Nazca Lines were made using simple tools.

____

4 **Answer the question with your own ideas.**

What do you think? How were the Nazca Lines made?

____

____

____

PRONUNCIATION

Moving word stress Go to page 120.

DEVELOPING *Writing*

A blog entry explaining a mystery

1 INPUT **Read the blog and answer the questions.**

1 What is the mystery?

____

2 When and where did it happen?

____

3 Has it been solved?

____

BLOG | ABOUT | NEWS | ARCHIVES | CONTACT ME

What happened to Flight MH370?

Malaysian Airlines Flight MH370 took off from Kuala Lumpur airport in Malaysia on March 8, 2014. Forty minutes later, it had disappeared. Nothing has been heard of the plane or its 227 passengers and 12 crew since then, despite the biggest search in the history of air travel.

The disappearance of Flight MH370 is unexplained and people have come up with their own theories about what happened.

One suggestion is that the plane might have caught fire and crashed into the ocean. In fact, it was carrying over 200 kg of lithium batteries, which explode very easily.

A sudden loss of air pressure in the cabin would have killed everyone, including the pilots, and caused a crash. However, someone suggested that only the co-pilot survived and could have flown the plane until it crashed. 1 ______________ .

In a book about the mystery, a historian claims the plane must have vanished as the result of a remote cyber hijacking because it had important material or people onboard. Surely that can't be true!

2 ______________ people on social media liked the theory of another Bermuda Triangle in the Indian Ocean. They believe Flight MH370 must have disappeared in the same place where other planes had vanished before. 3 ______________

Some people even believe the plane was hijacked by aliens, 4 ______________ .

The most likely explanation is that there must have been a problem with the plane – 5 ______________ . Cracks had been found in other Boeing 777s, which could have caused the plane to break up.

6 ______________

2 ANALYZE **Blogs are usually informal in style. Complete the blanks (1–6) with the phrases (a–f). Sometimes there is more than one correct answer.**

a but I'm not a big believer in extraterrestrials
b but why?
c That's one of the weirdest things I've ever heard!
d That's what I think.
e What do you think really happened to Flight MH370?
f Millions of

3 **Match the phrases in Exercise 2 (a–f) with their functions (1–6).**

1 giving your own opinion ☐
2 explaining your opinion ☐
3 inviting other opinions ☐
4 using a superlative to say you don't believe it ☐
5 exaggeration ☐
6 responding to an unexplained theory ☐

4 **When trying to explain a mystery, we use modal verbs of deduction and conditionals. Underline all the examples of these forms in the article.**

5 PLAN **Do some research into a mystery in your country and make a plan. Make sure you include all the points below.**

- the facts
- possible explanations
- your opinion

6 PRODUCE **Write your blog entry (200 words). Use some of the phrases in Exercise 2 and your plan from Exercise 5. Make sure you include all the points from the checklist.**

✓ CHECKLIST

Use an informal style.
Use modal verbs of deduction and conditionals to suggest explanations.
Include your own opinions.
Invite your readers to comment.

LISTENING

1 9.03 **Listen to two dialogues. Match the sentences (a–d) to the dialogues (1–2)**

a Someone made a mistake. ☐
b Someone lost something. ☐
c The speakers are getting ready to travel. ☐
d The speakers are waiting for someone. ☐

2 9.03 **Listen again and choose the correct answers.**

1
a Eddie thinks the missing thing is *definitely* / *probably* in his room.
b His mom *advises* / *warns* him what to do with important things.
c They set off *earlier* / *later* than planned.

2
a Dylan *is* / *isn't* surprised that Jess isn't there.
b Dylan thinks it is *possible* / *impossible* that Jess has forgotten.
c Jess *must* / *couldn't* have understood the plan they'd made.

3 9.03 **Complete these parts of the dialogues with *should(n't) have* and a verb in the list. Then listen and check.**

go | keep | rush | tell

1

Eddie I must have put it in a safe place, but I can't remember where.
Mom You [1] ______________________ it with your other important things, like your wallet and phone.
Mom OK, so, when did you last have it?
Eddie Last night! I had it in my hand, I remember. Ah, I [2] ______________________ so much!

2

Tanya You [3] ______________________ her to be here at seven – you know she's always late.
Dylan You're right, but she should be here by now.
Dylan You won't believe it! She's waiting for us outside the café.
Tanya She [4] ______________________ there! We're going there after the movie.

DIALOGUE

4 **Put the missing lines in the correct places to make three short dialogues.**

1

Lewis Have you seen the TV remote, Adam?
Adam ______________________
Lewis ______________________
Adam ______________________
Lewis ______________________

2

Beth Any news from the police on the missing Picasso painting?
Fraser ______________________
Beth ______________________
Fraser ______________________
Beth ______________________

3

Polly My bike. Someone stole it!
Chris ______________________
Polly ______________________
Chris ______________________
Polly ______________________

1 So try the dog basket – Spike might have taken it.
2 Stole it. Are you sure?
3 Well, it was long enough for them to break the lock. I don't believe it!
4 Well, let's hope they arrest someone soon and find the painting.
5 I think it must have been someone who worked at the gallery.
6 Of course I'm sure. I left it locked up just here.
7 That's a good idea. I'll go and have a look.
8 No, I haven't. It's probably down the side of the sofa. That's where it usually is.
9 They can't have gone far – we were only in the store for five minutes.
10 I've already searched the whole sofa. It isn't there.
11 No, they don't even know how the robber got into the building.
12 Yes, I think you're right. Someone who knew how to turn off the alarm.

5 **Use one of the lines below to start or end a five-line dialogue.**

1 You shouldn't have done that!
2 You should have told me right away.
3 It must have been my sister.
4 It couldn't have been easy.

LISTENING
Sentence completion

EXAM GUIDE

You will listen to a monologue, such as a talk, a presentation or part of a radio programme. While you are listening, you have to complete ten sentences using the information you hear in the recording.

Before you listen ...

- read the title and the text as these will prepare you for what you are going to hear.
- look carefully at the words **before** and **after** the gaps.
- think about the type of information you need to complete each sentence.
- underline the key words.

While you listen ...

- remember the questions follow the same order as the recording.
- you must only write **one**, **two** or **three** words in each gap.
- focus carefully on the details.
- you will hear the **exact word(s)** you need to complete the gaps in the recording.
- read the completed sentences to make sure they make sense.

1 9.04 **You will hear Gaby talking about an unforgettable school trip to the ancient monument of Stonehenge in south-west England. For questions 1–10, complete the sentences with a word or short phrase.**

SCHOOL TRIP

The visit to Stonehenge was the [1]________________ of Gaby's trip to the UK.

The first thing that impressed her about Stonehenge was its [2]________________ .

It's estimated that work started on Stonehenge about [3]________________ years ago.

The stones that were used in the [4]________________ of construction came from mountains in Wales.

The biggest stones were so heavy that they must have been [5]________________ there on tree trunks.

Gaby says Stonehenge is [6]________________ other ancient monuments because the reason it was built is still a mystery.

People come here to see the [7]________________ on the longest and shortest days of the year.

It might have been used for observing [8]________________ of stars in the night sky.

Another theory is that it was a type of [9]________________ that showed the passing hours by the position of the sunlight on the stones.

Gaby doesn't believe the monument was constructed by [10]________________ .

10 MONEY

GRAMMAR

Future continuous

→ SB p.94

1 ★☆☆ Put the words in order to make sentences. Use the future continuous.

This time next year, ...

0 my / host / cooking show / grandma / on TV / a

My grandma will be hosting a cooking show on TV.

1 dad / my / race / the / in / Grand Prix

____

2 sister / work / children's home / Cambodia / in / my / at / a

____

3 brother / my / sail / world / the / around

____

4 mom / act / my / in / a / production / theater

____

5 cousin / research / my / cancer / cure / a / for

____

6 best friend / travel / South Africa / to / my

____

7 I / human rights / a / lawyer / famous / work / as

____

2 ★★★ What do you think will be happening 50 years from now? Use the ideas in parentheses to write sentences in the future continuous.

0 (type of transportation / travel)

People will be traveling in computer-controlled flying cars.

1 (phones / use)

____

2 (money / use)

____

3 (school textbooks / use)

____

4 (houses / live)

____

3 ★★★ Write fantasy predictions for your friends and family. Use the future continuous.

Ten years from now, ...

1 my ______________________________

2 my ______________________________

3 my ______________________________

4 my ______________________________

5 my ______________________________

6 I ______________________________

Future perfect

→ SB p.97

4 ★☆☆ Complete the conversation with the future perfect tense of the verbs in parentheses.

Mom Have you done your homework yet?

Kyle No, but I [1] ________________ (finish) it by the time Dad gets home.

Mom Have you cleaned your room yet?

Kyle No, but I [2] ________________ (clean) it by bedtime.

Mom Have you fed the cat yet?

Kyle No, but I [3] ________________ (feed) it by 6 p.m.

Mom Have you done that essay yet?

Kyle No, but I [4] ________________ (write) it by this time tomorrow.

Mom And have you prepared dinner yet?

Kyle No, but I [5] ________________ (make) it by the time everyone gets hungry.

5 ★★☆ **Complete the conversation with the future perfect of the verbs in the list.**

become | bike | buy | find
finish | go | move | not have
sail | see | swim | travel

Yuri What plans do you have for the future, Penny?

Penny Me? By 2030, I [1] ______ college, and I [2] ______ to New York. I [3] ______ an amazing apartment there, and I [4] ______ a successful architect.

Yuri Wow!

Penny What about you? [5] ______ you ______ around the world? You always said you'd like to do that.

Yuri Of course. I [6] ______ across the English Channel, and I [7] ______ across the Atlantic Ocean. I [8] ______ across China, and I [9] ______ the pyramids in Mexico and Guatemala. Oh, and of course, I [10] ______ kayaking down the Grand Canyon.

Penny [11] ______ a job?

Yuri No, I [12] ______ time to find a job!

Future perfect and future continuous

6 ★★☆ **Complete the predictions with the future perfect or the future continuous.**

1 By 2030, internet use ______ (reach) 7.5 billion worldwide.
2 By 2040, smoking in public ______ (be) banned in every US state.
3 By 2050, robots ______ (work) in factories instead of humans.
4 By 2060, people ______ (use) telepathy to communicate.
5 By 2070, nearly half the Amazon rainforest ______ (be) cut down.
6 By 2080, scientists ______ (invent) invisibility suits.
7 By 2090, people ______ (drive) flying cars.
8 By 2100, many of the world's languages ______ (disappear).

7 ★★☆ **Complete the text with the future perfect or the future continuous of the verbs in the list.**

become | build | eat | explore
live | produce | ~~travel~~

By 2050, I don't think people [0] *will have traveled* to Mars. However, I think they [1] ______ space. Some people [2] ______ in space stations, because the Earth [3] ______ too crowded.
I think scientists [4] ______ huge farms in space in special glass buildings, and they [5] ______ very healthy food for everyone. People [6] ______ specially developed fruit and vegetables.

8 ★★★ **Write goals for yourself. Complete the sentences using the future perfect or future continuous.**

1 By tomorrow evening, I ______
2 By next week, ______
3 By next year, ______
4 By the time I'm 20, ______
5 By the time I'm 50, ______

GET IT RIGHT!

Future perfect vs. future simple

Learners often confuse the future perfect with the future simple.

✓ *By the end of next year, I will have finished my studies.*
✗ *By the end of next year, I ~~will finish~~ my studies.*

Complete the sentences with the verb in parentheses in the correct form: future perfect or future simple.

0 I *will have gone back* to Beijing by June. (go)
1 We hope you ______ to our party next weekend. (come)
2 I'd really like that game – maybe my parents ______ it for my birthday. (buy)
3 By the time I finish my English course, my skills ______ a lot. (improve)
4 I promise I ______ there at 5 p.m. tomorrow. (be)
5 We hope that in a week's time we ______ all our exams! (finish)
6 By this time tomorrow, they ______ in Australia. (arrive)

VOCABULARY

Money and value

→ SB p.94

1 ★★☆ **Complete the sentences with the words and phrases in the list. There are three you don't need.**

bargain | refund | off | sale
owe | reward | tip | valuable
value for money | worth

1 This ruby ring is very ________________ . My great-grandmother gave it to my mom.
2 My grandpa's stamp collection is ________________ a lot of money now.
3 I ________________ Jack some money. I borrowed $10 from him last week.
4 These sneakers are usually over $50. I got them for $20. They were a real ________________ .
5 We got the tent for half price. I think it's very good ________________ .
6 The store owner gave me a ________________ for catching the shoplifter.
7 There's a winter sale at the sporting goods store – $10 ________________ everything!

2 ★☆☆ **Complete the dialogue with some of the words and phrases in Exercise 1.**

Felix Is that a new bike you have there?
Leonie Yeah! It's really cool and I only paid $100 for it.
Felix $100! That's a [1]________________ . It's [2]________________ a lot more than that.
Leonie Yes, it was on [3]________________ – $75 [4]________________ .
Felix That's great [5]________________ money.
Leonie The only problem is I now [6]________________ my parents $50. I only had $50 in savings, so they lent me the rest of the money.

Jobs and work

→ SB p.97

3 ★☆☆ **Circle the correct words.**

1 My dad works in *healthcare* / *finance*. He's a nurse.
2 What *management* / *qualifications* do you need to be an air traffic controller?
3 I've been an *employee* / *employer* of SmartArt for ten years now.
4 Ms. Brown is my *employer* / *employee*. I've worked for her company for 15 years now.
5 Peter has a *finance* / *management* job now – he has a team of people working under him.
6 She does scientific experiments for the government; she works in *finance* / *public service*.

4 ★★☆ **Match the sentences.**

1 I'm a bank employee. ☐
2 I work as a consultant in a hospital. ☐
3 I am a principal at an elementary school in Maryland. ☐
4 I have a job in a government office. ☐
5 I want to be a Supreme Court judge. ☐

a I work in education.
b I work in public service.
c I work in finance.
d I'm studying law at the university.
e I work in healthcare.

WordWise: Phrases with *by*

→ SB p.95

5 **Read the four sentences. In which sentence is *by* used …**

1 to say how something is done? ☐
2 to say where something is? ☐
3 to say when something is/will be done? ☐
4 to say who does something? ☐

a There's no traffic today, so I think we'll get there by nine o'clock.
b I bought these shoes at that new store by the supermarket.
c This photo was taken by my grandmother.
d I bought my new computer by saving up for six months!

6 **Complete the sentences.**

by working | by a friend | by ten o'clock
by my bedroom door | by Monday
by practicing

1 This book was written ________________ of my teacher's.
2 We have three days to do the homework – the teacher said he wants it ________________ .
3 I learned to play the guitar ________________ for two hours every day.
4 James made some money ________________ in a café on the weekends.
5 Our cat always sleeps ________________ .
6 The movie starts at 8 p.m., so I'm sure it will have finished ________________ .

REFERENCE

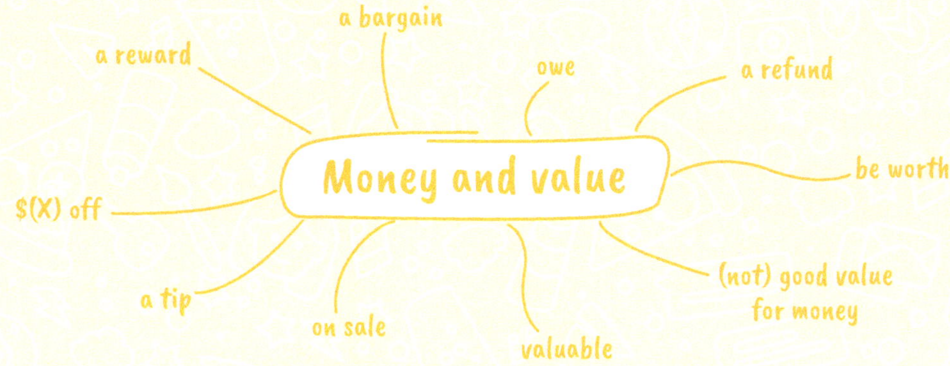

PHRASES WITH *BY*

by alternative payment methods (the person/people/things that do something)

by answering (a way to do something)

by the entrance (a location)

by 2035 (a time in the future)

VOCABULARY *EXTRA*

1 Match the words and phrases in the list to their meanings.

debt | scholarship | have a positive balance
loan | payment | savings

1 money given by an organization for a special purpose, e.g., to study a course ________________
2 an amount of money you spend for a particular thing ________________
3 an amount of money you borrow, often from a bank ________________
4 having money available in your bank account ________________
5 money you don't spend, but keep for later ________________
6 money that you owe someone ________________

2 Complete the sentences with the words and phrases in Exercise 1.

1 My sister received a ________________ to go to college.
2 I'm going to use my ________________ to go on a trip with my friends.
3 Matthew owed me $20, but he paid off his ________________ when he got his wages.
4 My mom made the ________________ for the tickets by credit card.
5 My parents got a ________________ from the bank to buy our house.
6 Now that Kieran has a job, his bank account ________________ .

3 Answer the questions with your own ideas.

1 Do students get scholarships in your country?
____
____
____

2 In your country, which types of payment are most popular?
____
____
____

3 Do you think it's important to pay off debts as soon as you can?
____
____
____

4 Do you think it's important to have savings? Why?
____
____
____

READING

1 **Read the article and match the questions (a–g) with the paragraphs (1–7).**

a What are the advantages?
b What are community currencies exactly?
c Are they the same as national currency?
d Are community currencies successful?
e Why does a town need its own money?
f What's the future for community currencies?
g How do they work?

2 **Read the article again and match the parts of the sentences.**

1 A community currency belongs ☐
2 The main advantage is that ☐
3 Businesses can decide ☐
4 Community currencies make ☐
5 Most community currency projects ☐
6 Local money projects will be ☐

a to join the project or not.
b work very well.
c it improves the financial situation.
d expanding over the next few years.
e to a single town or area.
f people's lives better in many ways.

3 CRITICAL THINKING **Read the article again and match a possible disadvantage to Paragraph 1–6. Can you think of any other disadvantages?**

Paragraph 1	☐	Paragraph 4	☐
Paragraph 2	☐	Paragraph 5	☐
Paragraph 3	☐	Paragraph 6	☐

a People might prefer to pay by cash in local stores.
b It can't be used everywhere.
c You can't use the money for saving.
d It doesn't help the national economy.
e You have less choice if you only buy local products.
f Not all stores and businesses accept the local money.

LOCAL MONEY

The dollar, pound, euro, peso, and yen are well-known world currencies, but have you heard of the Bristol Pound, the Abeille, or the Urstromtaler? Probably not, because these currencies are only used in single towns. They are all examples of community currencies.

1 ________________ ?

A community currency is money that can only be spent in one particular place. It doesn't replace the national currency – it is used as an alternative instead. For example, in the city of Bristol in the UK, people can pay for their shopping in pounds sterling (£) or in Bristol pounds (£B).

2 ________________ ?

The aim of a community currency is to help the town's economy. It encourages residents to support businesses in the area so that the money stays in the local community. In this way, businesses grow, attract new customers, and create new jobs, which makes the economy stronger.

3 ________________ ?

First, the town has to set up a community interest company. This company holds a sum of national currency and prints money in the community currency. Businesses join the project by agreeing to accept these bills as payment from customers. People who are paid in local money or get it as change can spend it in the stores and businesses that are part of the project.

4 ________________ ?

There's one important difference between national and local money: local bills have a spend-by date printed on them and if the bills aren't spent before this date, they become worthless. Community currencies work better if the money is being used actively rather than saved.

5 ________________ ?

Towns that have tried this experiment have found a lot of benefits. Having their own currency brings the community together, which creates a positive identity. People who are proud of their town get involved in new projects, such as organizing events and charity work. Thinking locally is not only good for the economy, but also for the environment. By buying local products, you save energy and reduce pollution. The local currency also helps local stores compete against the multinationals by encouraging people to buy from them instead of from big supermarkets and chains.

6 ________________ ?

The numbers speak for themselves: in Bristol, over £B 5 million were spent in the first six years of the project. Bristol's residents can pay for public transportation, services, shopping, and even local taxes using community money. There are over 10,000 community currencies around the world, and more are being planned.

7 ________________ ?

The world is moving towards a cashless society. It is predicted that paper money and coins will have disappeared before the end of the century in many countries. Community currencies will be playing an important part in the cashless world. Community interest companies have been following current trends by creating apps for digital payments. Experts are hoping that this user-friendly, cheap technology will soon be helping communities in the developing world to create community currencies that will bring them the benefits they need.

DEVELOPING *Writing*

An essay

1 INPUT **Read Ava's essay. Circle the correct options.**

1 Overall, Ava thinks the statement in the title is *true / false.*
2 When Ava writes "I really envy them," she's *agreeing / disagreeing* with the title.
3 When Ava writes "I'd rather go camping ...," she's *agreeing / disagreeing* with the title.

Time to enjoy life is more important than earning a lot of money

Both my parents have successful careers in the finance industry and are very well paid, but they're hardly ever at home. They earn a lot of money, but they don't have much time to enjoy life. My friend Grace's family doesn't have as much money as us, but they have a lot of fun doing things together. I really envy them.

First, people who have high salaries often don't have time to spend their money because they are working all the time. **Secondly**, they spend more time at work than with their families and they don't have much energy for free-time activities either. When my mom and dad are at home, they're so tired, they just relax.

Without doubt, a good salary gives you security because you don't have any money worries. You are able to buy everything you and your family need. In addition, you have probably reached the top of your career and your job is interesting and gives you a lot of satisfaction. But will you be happy? What's more, will your family be happy?

On the one hand, money makes you wealthy, but on the other, it makes you time-poor. My parents can take us on fantastic vacations and give us presents. **However**, they can't give us the time we would like with them. I'd rather go on camping trips over the summer like Grace's family. **For these reasons**, I believe that a high salary is definitely not as important as having time to spend with your family.

2 **Match the words in bold in the essay with the words with similar meanings (a–d). Then find three other linking words or phrases in the essay.**

a but 1 ____________
b furthermore 2 ____________
c therefore 3 ____________
d without question 4 ____________

____________, ____________, ____________

3 ANALYZE **Put the statements in order to make Ava's essay plan.**

☐ a conclusion
☐ b introduction stating my opinion
☐ c the first argument against the statement
☐ d the first argument for the statement
☐ e the second argument against the statement
☐ f the second argument for the statement

4 **Look at the text again and underline the examples Ava gives to support her ideas.**

5 PLAN **You are going to write an essay with the title: *Money isn't the most important thing in the world.* Complete the plan with your ideas.**

Introduction	
Arguments for the statement	
Arguments against the statement	
Conclusion	

6 PRODUCE **Write your essay (200–250 words). Use your plan from Exercise 5. Make sure you include all the points in the checklist.**

✓ CHECKLIST

Write in a formal style.
Organize your essay into paragraphs.
Use linking words to join your ideas.
Give examples to support your ideas.

LISTENING

1 10.01 **Listen to the dialogue between Libby and Brad. Match the plans (a–d) with the people.**

Libby ☐ ☐ Brad ☐ ☐

a do a sports program
b go to a concert
c improve a skill
d look for a job

2 10.01 **Listen again and mark the sentences T (true) or F (false). Then correct the false sentences.**

1 Libby couldn't go away with her friends because she had to work. ☐
2 She has started saving her money for a future event. ☐
3 Brad's going to the music festival with Louis. ☐
4 Brad will probably do the same summer job as last year. ☐
5 Libby's parents hope she'll become a professional dancer. ☐
6 Libby's certain her parents will let her go to France if she gets a place in the course. ☐

DIALOGUE

3 10.01 **Listen again and complete these parts of the dialogue.**

Brad Are you alone?
Libby Yeah, my friends all are at the music festival. I [1]________________ customers at the café all day tomorrow while they [2]________________ and enjoying the festival.
Brad [3]________________ . Why didn't you go with them?
Libby I didn't have enough money for the ticket.
Brad [4]________________ , you can go next year.

Brad OK, I suppose it isn't that bad. You get in shape and you can earn a lot if you work on weekends. Maybe I'll just do that because if I don't earn some money, I [5]________________ and then I won't be able to go on vacation with my friends.
Libby Wow! Without your parents?
Brad Yes, first time! We'll be spending the last week of August camping on the beach.
Libby Lucky you!
Brad The place has a surf school and by the end of the week, we [6]________________ to surf – with a bit of luck!
Libby Cool! I wish I was doing something exciting this summer. I wanted to go to a summer camp in Boston, but I [7]________________ now.
Brad [8]________________ !

PHRASES FOR FLUENCY

→ SB p.98

4 **Complete the phrases. Then match them with the phrases that are similar.**

1 s_m_ _s _s_ _l ☐
2 D_n't l_ _k _t m_! ☐
3 _'m br_ke ☐
4 _r_ _n m_ ☐
5 th_t's _ll ☐
6 _t's n_t my f_ _lt ☐

a I have no money.
b I didn't do it!
c There's no difference.
d I will pay for them!
e Someone else did it!
f I only meant …

5 **Now complete the dialogues with some of the phrases in Exercise 4.**

1
A Hi, Joe. You seem really busy these days. I haven't seen you around!
B Oh, it's the [1]________________________ . Too much to do and not enough time!
A Well, tell me if you want to hang out.
B No, not today, sorry.
A Sure, I was worried about you, [2]________________________ .

2
A Are you coming for an ice cream?
B I can't. [3]________________________ .
A Don't worry. The ice creams [4]________________________ . My grandpa gave me some money for cutting the grass in his yard.
B Cool! Thanks!

3
A What's happened to my phone? The screen shattered!
B [5]________________________ ! A girl walked by and her bag knocked it onto the floor.
A But you should have moved it for me!
B [6]________________________ ! You shouldn't have left it on the edge of the table!

PRONUNCIATION
Short and long vowel sounds: /ɪ/ – /iː/ and /ɑ/ – /oʊ/ Go to page 121.

WRITING
An essay

EXAM GUIDE

For this part of the test, you have to write an essay. You are given the title of the essay and some notes to use. Two of the notes are already completed, but you have to think of an idea for the third note.

- Read the question and the notes carefully.
- Write a short plan.
- Organise your essay into paragraphs.
- You have about 40 minutes to write your answer to Part 1.

In Justin's English class, they have been discussing education. Their teacher has asked them to write an essay for homework.

Write your essay using all the notes and giving reasons for your point of view.

Write 140–190 words.

Secondary schools should offer vocational courses – courses that train you for a job.

Notes

Write about:

1 skills for work
2 benefits of university
3 ______________ (your own idea)

1 Read Justin's notes (a–f) for his essay. Which point, 1 or 2, in the essay question does each note belong to?

Secondary schools should offer vocational courses

Most schools prepare students for university, but they don't prepare them for a job.
However, there are many school-leavers who decide to start work straightaway. These students would benefit from vocational courses which give them practical qualifications.
These courses should be offered as an alternative to academic lessons. Firstly, many students prefer practical work to studying. Vocational courses would motivate them to work harder.
Most importantly, they are good for students who find it hard to study and sit quietly in class. However, vocational courses are often difficult for schools to organise because they need special teachers and expensive equipment.
Students who enjoy studying should still try for university. Parents often believe that a degree leads to a better job. University prepares young people for life by giving them opportunities to meet different people and try new experiences.
University isn't for everybody. There are other interesting careers that don't require a degree.
Therefore, I think vocational courses should be included in the school curriculum.

a suitable for students who prefer learning practical skills – not studying ☐
b good for students who like studying ☐
c can learn about different jobs, for example: computer programming, hairdressing ☐
d learn a useful skill for work ☐
e an experience that prepares you for the future in many ways ☐
f adults think a university degree gives more opportunities for a career ☐

2 Read Justin's essay again. What is his own idea for point 3?

3 Read the exam question and write your essay.

In your English class you have been talking about parents who choose to teach their children at home instead of sending them to school. Your teacher has asked you to write an essay for homework.

Write your essay using all the notes and giving reasons for your point of view.

Writer 140–190 words.

Some children never go to school because their parents teach them at home. Do you think this is a good idea?

Notes

Write about:

1 lessons
2 making friends
3 ______________ (your own idea)

4 Ask a friend to read your essay and complete the sentences about it.

I thought the essay was ______________ .
The ideas you included were ______________ .
The language used was ______________ .
You could improve it by ______________ .

CONSOLIDATION

LISTENING

1 10.04 **Listen to the dialogue between Rob and Carrie. Write the prices of these items and check (✓) the ones that Rob bought.**

1 $______

3 $______

2 $______

4 $______

2 10.04 **Listen again and mark the sentences T (true) or F (false).**

1 Rob thinks he's missing $18.
2 He put $10 of credit on his phone.
3 Rob stopped at the ice cream shop after the bookstore.
4 Carrie suggests that someone could have taken his money.
5 Rob asks Carrie to buy him a movie ticket.
6 Matt lends Rob $5.

GRAMMAR

3 **Circle the correct options.**

1 You shouldn't *say* / *have said* that. She's really upset now.
2 She always travels by bike. She must *be* / *have been* fit.
3 This time next week I'll *be lying* / *have been lying* on a beach in the Caribbean.
4 They'll *be* / *have been* married for 20 years in December.
5 You spent too much. You should *be* / *have been* more careful with money.
6 No one passed the test. It can't *be* / *have been* very easy.
7 If it keeps on raining like this, we won't *have played* / *be playing* tennis at three o'clock.
8 This time next year, I will *be studying* / *have studied* English for four years.

4 **Complete the sentences with two words.**

1 By the time he comes back home, my brother ________________ visited 20 countries.
2 This time next week, I'll ________________ breakfast in a hotel in Miami.
3 They look very tired. They ________________ worked very hard today.
4 You're late! You ________________ arrived 30 minutes ago!
5 Someone told me they lost 7–1! They ________________ played very well.

VOCABULARY

5 **Match the parts of the sentences.**

1 The crime remains unexplained,
2 Henry hasn't replied to my email,
3 When their team won the game,
4 Several people reported seeing a strange
5 It isn't very valuable. It can't be
6 If you aren't happy, you can bring it
7 There was $25 off this coat on sale,
8 You have to buy it. It's only on

a their fans went crazy.
b back to the store and get a refund.
c so it was a real bargain.
d sale for today.
e and to this day, nobody knows what really happened.
f worth more than $50.
g man running from the crime scene.
h which is really puzzling.

6 **Complete each word.**

1 That's o_ _ – I left my gym bag here five minutes ago and now it's gone.
2 I only paid $3 – it was a real b_ _ _ _ _ _ _ .
3 There's a r_ _ _ _ _ of $20 for finding the missing cat.
4 I'll tell you, but it's a s_ _ _ _ _ and I don't want you to tell anybody.
5 I'm not going to leave the waiter a t_ _ . The service was terrible.
6 Scientists believe the rock is e_ _ _ _ _ _ _ _ _ _ _ _ _ _ _ _ and came from another planet.
7 She definitely works in h_ _ _ _ _ _ _ _ _ _ . She's either a dentist or a doctor.
8 At only $200, it's really good v_ _ _ _ for money.

DIALOGUE

7 10.05 **Complete the dialogue with the phrases in the list. There are two you don't need. Then listen and check.**

more than likely | you must be joking | a shame
forget about it | same as usual | goes without saying
don't look at me | how awful

Milo I don't believe it. Someone spilled soda all over my project.

Becky 1________________. I had nothing to do with it.

Yildiz It was John, 2________________. He's really clumsy.

Milo Well, it 3________________ that I'm not at all happy about it. It's ruined. Look at it.

Becky 4________________. Can't you do it again?

Milo 5________________. It took me three days and it has to be handed in tomorrow.

Yildiz That's 6________________. You'll just have to tell the teacher what happened and ask for some more time.

Milo I only hope he'll agree. Just wait until I see John.

READING

8 **Read the article and answer the questions.**

1 How did the boys find out how the machine worked?

____

2 Why didn't anyone at the bank believe their story?

____

3 What evidence did the boys take back to the bank?

____

4 What else did they do to show they had hacked into the machine?

____

5 Why did the bank manager write them a note?

____

WRITING

9 **Write a paragraph of about 150–200 words on your thoughts about money. Include this information.**

- how you get money
- what you spend it on
- anything you're saving up for
- ways you could get more money

HONEST TEENS IN CASH MACHINE SCANDAL

When Matthew Hewlett and Caleb Turon decided to try to hack into an ATM, they could hardly have imagined how easy it would be. The two 14-year-old Canadians had found a manual explaining how to operate the Bank of Montreal ATM online. In the manual, there was a password. One day during their lunch break from school, they decided to try out the password at the machine in their local supermarket. To their surprise, the six-digit password took them straight into the machine's computer, where they were able to access all the data it contained.

The boys went straight to the closest branch of the Bank of Montreal, where they told a cashier what had happened. She immediately told her colleagues, who refused to believe the boys, saying that it was impossible. They said that they couldn't have hacked into the machine and that they had no evidence to support their story. So the boys asked if it would be alright if they got some proof. The bank staff agreed that they could, but told them they would never be able to get anything out of the ATM.

The boys returned to the machine and hacked it once again. This time they printed out information such as all the cash withdrawals that had been made that day and how much money was in the machine. They also changed the welcome message on the screen to: "Go away. This machine has been hacked."

They returned to the bank with the evidence, and this time they were taken seriously. The manager of the bank came to thank them personally. He even wrote them a note to show to their teachers explaining why they were so late coming back from their lunch break!

11 EMERGENCY!

GRAMMAR

Verbs followed by gerund or infinitive

→ SB p.104

1 ★★☆ Put the words in order to make sentences.

1 mind / I / you / helping / don't

____

2 You / buy / can't / it / afford / to

____

3 promised / tomorrow / to / tell / He / us

____

4 don't / They / see / their car / expect / again / to

____

5 She / to / café / suggested / the / going

____

6 favorite / Imagine / movie star / meeting / your

____

2 ★★☆ Complete the sentences with the gerund or infinitive form of the verbs in parentheses.

There are some beautiful hills near where we live and we enjoy [1]________________ (walk) there on the weekends. But we learned [2]________________ (be) careful and [3]________________ (tell) people where we are going. Usually we avoid [4]________________ (go) up there if the weather is going to be bad.

But one day we decided [5]________________ (go) up, even though we'd heard it might get foggy. We really wanted [6]________________ (get) some exercise. So we set off – the weather was nice and sunny, and everything was great. We didn't expect [7]________________ (have) any problems.

After two hours, we felt like [8]________________ (take) a break, so we sat down. And then the fog started coming in.

My wife suggested [9]________________ (go) back immediately, but I wanted [10]________________ (stay) a bit longer. Big mistake! Soon we couldn't see anything – we didn't know which way to go at all. My wife called the emergency services. Twenty minutes later, they found us and helped us back home.

I had never imagined [11]________________ (need) to make an emergency phone call. And I have promised myself never [12]________________ (go) into the hills again when the weather forecast isn't good.

3 ★★★ Complete each sentence with the correct form of a verb from each list.

afford | avoid | feel like | miss | ~~offer~~ | practice | promise

buy | eat | give | ~~lend~~ | live | speak | study

0 My brother *offered to lend* me his laptop today so I can do some work.

1 Let's go to the Indian restaurant. I ________________ a nice hot curry!

2 Tickets for the concert are really expensive. I can't ________________ one.

3 We don't like this city. We really ________________ in the country, like we used to.

4 Lily ________________ me her answer tomorrow. I hope she says yes.

5 My friends love going to France, because they can ________________ French.

6 Jonah always ________________ the night before a test.

PRONUNCIATION

Strong and weak forms: /tuː/ and /tə/

Go to page 121.

to / *in order to* / *so as to*

→ SB p.105

4 ★☆☆ Choose the correct options.

Patrick and his friends were really happy because they'd gotten tickets for the big baseball game. They had lined up for three hours the week before [1]*to / not to* get the tickets.

The boys got to the stadium early, [2]*so as to / so as not to* have to stand in a long line. On the way, they stopped at a store [3]*in order to / in order not to* buy some food and drinks – they bought a lot [4]*so as not to / so as to* feel hungry in the middle of the game.

While they were waiting for the game to start, the sun came out and they took their sweatshirts off [5]*to / to not* get too hot. And then the game began! Unfortunately, a couple of really big, tall guys sat in front of them, so sometimes the boys had to stand up [6]*to / not to* see what was happening. But after about an hour, the men left, so for the rest of the game Patrick and his friends had a perfect view.

5 ★★☆ **Make the two sentences into one using the words in parentheses.**

0 I got up at 6 a.m. I wanted to get some good photographs. (in order to)
I got up at 6 a.m. in order to get some good photographs.

1 The girls got to the lake early. They wanted to get a place in the shade. (so as to)
____

2 I called Michelle. I wanted to invite her to my party. (to)
____

3 Lachlan didn't tell his parents about the accident. He didn't want to worry them. (so as not to)
____

4 We took the train. We didn't want to get hot biking. (in order not to)
____

5 Mae would like to talk to her. She wants to apologize. (in order to)
____

6 Are you saving your money? You want to buy a new laptop. (so as to)
____

so and *such*

→ SB p.107

6 ★☆☆ **Circle the correct words.**

1 Samuel was *so* / *such* tired that he just wanted to go to bed.
2 They were *so* / *such* difficult questions that no one could answer them.
3 The water was *so* / *such* cold that we couldn't stay in the pool for more than five minutes!
4 The team drank *so* / *such* much water that we had to get some more.
5 I've lived here *so* / *such* a long time that I can't remember living anywhere else.
6 The concert tickets were *so* / *such* expensive that we couldn't afford them.

7 ★★☆ **Complete the sentences with *so* or *such a*.**

1 I need to take an aspirin. I have ______________ bad headache.
2 I was ______________ scared that I couldn't move.
3 The food was ______________ hot that we had to wait before eating it.
4 Julia told ______________ funny joke we couldn't stop laughing.
5 Giorgio was awarded a medal because he had done ______________ brave thing.
6 I'm ______________ worried about the exam tomorrow.

8 ★★★ **Read the sentence pairs. Write a new (third) sentence so that it has the same meaning as the sentence pair. Use *so* and *such*.**

0 I'm really hungry. I'm going to eat another sandwich.
I'm so hungry that I'm going to eat another sandwich.

1 Maddie's really friendly. I always like being with her.
____

2 The boys left very early. They were gone before lunch.
____

3 I have a bad stomachache. I might go home.
____

4 It was a terrible movie. We left before the end.
____

5 The teacher's explanation was complicated. We couldn't understand it.
____

6 The party was a great success. We're going to have another one next week.
____

GET IT RIGHT!

Verbs with *to* + base form

With verbs that require *to* + base form, we do not use *for* (+ *to*) + base form.

✓ *I went to the movie theater to see a movie.*
✗ *I went to the movie theater ~~for to see~~ a movie.*

We can use *for* + noun.

✓ *I bought some chocolates for his birthday.*
✗ *I bought some chocolates ~~for to give~~ him.*
✓ *I bought some chocolates to give him.*

Check (✓) the correct sentences. Correct the incorrect ones.

1 I'm here for English lessons. ☐
____
2 You need to turn on the light for to see better. ☐
____
3 He uses his tablet for to read books. ☐
____
4 I use my phone for taking photos. ☐
____
5 I asked you to give me information. ☐
____
6 Giraffes have a long neck for to reach the tops of trees. ☐
____

VOCABULARY
Danger and safety

→ SB p.104

1 ★★☆ Complete the sentences.

1 He was very sick, but now the doctors say that he's o__________ of danger.
2 I can't thank you enough – you s__________ my life!
3 Don't go in there – it's very d__________ .
4 All the passengers s__________ the crash thanks to the driver's fast thinking.
5 The firefighters found a man in the burning house and pulled him to s__________ .
6 Their boat sank, but they were r__________ by a passing ship.
7 When we saw the water coming, we knew we were in d__________ , so we ran to higher ground as fast as we could.
8 After two weeks in the hospital, she finally r__________ and was allowed to go home.

2 ★★☆ Complete the story with a word or phrase in Exercise 1.

I could see that I was in a very [1]__________ situation. I was trying to [2]__________ the princess's life, but her enemies were getting very close. Now both of us were [3]__________ .

I looked around – how could we escape? There was an open window, but we were on the fifth floor. I looked down – we could jump, but I didn't know if we would [4]__________ the fall. But there were no other options – jumping was the only way that we could get to [5]__________ .

I turned to the princess. She looked at me. "Thank you," she said. "I've been a prisoner here so long. Thank you for coming to [6]__________ me." I smiled. "No problem, your Highness," I said. "But we're not [7]__________ yet, I'm afraid."

The princess looked out of the window. "OK," she said. "Let's jump. If we get hurt, there's a chance we'll [8]__________ before too long."

I thought: "How brave she is!" We went to the window. We held hands and …

"Danny!" said my mom. "Time for dinner. And stop playing that computer game!"

Adjectives with negative prefixes

→ SB p.107

3 ★☆☆ Write the negative forms of the words.

1 happy	__________	6 necessary	__________
2 expensive	__________	7 legal	__________
3 possible	__________	8 formal	__________
4 comfortable	__________	9 patient	__________
5 true	__________	10 polite	__________

4 ★★☆ Complete the sentences with the words in Exercise 3.

1 Your little sister's crying – she must be __________ about something.
2 You don't have to dress up – it's an __________ party.
3 Please don't leave without saying goodbye – it's __________ .
4 Lunch will be ready in a few minutes – don't be so __________ !
5 No one can pick up 400 kilograms – it's __________ !
6 I didn't sleep well – the bed was very __________ .
7 It's only $5.99 – it's __________ .
8 They didn't need to have all that violence in the movie – it was really __________ .
9 No, I didn't take your backpack – that's completely __________ !
10 In my country, it's __________ to drive a car if you're under 18.

5 ★★★ Complete the conversation with the words in the list. There are two extra words.

danger | illegal | impolite | miracle
recovered | rescued | safety | saved
survived | tragedy | trapped
uncomfortable | unhappy | unnecessary

Arlo Look, Silvia, I really don't want to be [1]__________ , but can you put your seat belt on please?

Silvia But I hate wearing seat belts, they're very [2]__________ . And anyway, I'm in the back.

Arlo I'm sorry, but you have to. It's the law. It's [3]__________ not to wear a seat belt, even in the back.

Silvia Well, to be honest, I think if people drive carefully, then seat belts are [4]__________ .

Arlo I really don't agree. A friend of mine was in an accident and her seat belt [5]__________ her life. She was a passenger in the back seat of a car that crashed. It's a [6]__________ that she [7]__________ .

Silvia Really?

Arlo Yes, her leg was [8]__________ . She was in the car for almost an hour, but the fire service [9]__________ her. They took her to the hospital. Her life was in [10]__________ for almost 24 hours. But she [11]__________ OK, I'm happy to say. It was almost a [12]__________ , though.

Silvia OK, you've convinced me. I'm going to wear a seat belt from now on!

REFERENCE

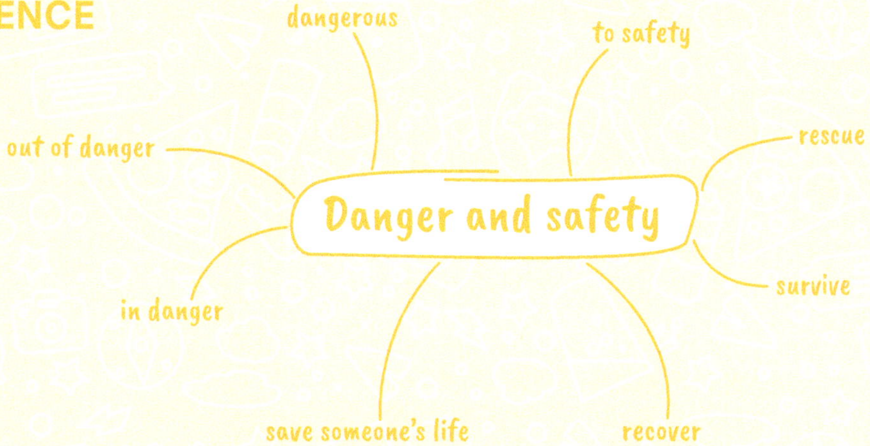

ADJECTIVES WITH NEGATIVE PREFIXES

il-	im-	in-	ir-	un-
illegal	impatient	inexpensive	irregular	unafraid
illogical	impolite	informal	irresponsible	uncomfortable
	impossible			unconcerned
				unhappy
				unhealthy
				unhelpful
				unimportant
				unnecessary
				unsurprising
				untrue

VOCABULARY *EXTRA*

1 **Choose a word or phrase from the list that could replace each word in bold.**

hurt | not dangerous | possibly dangerous
silly | safe | very frightening

1 Rabbits are **harmless**, so they make good pets.

____

2 If you concentrate more, you won't make so many **careless** mistakes.

____

3 Rock climbing is a **risky** sport.

____

4 The door is locked and windows are closed, so the room is **secure**.

____

5 When Jack fell off his skateboard, he **injured** his arm.

____

6 The dark cave was **terrifying**. I couldn't wait to get out!

____

2 **Circle the correct words.**

1 Luckily, we weren't *injured* / *careless* in the accident.
2 Being out in that storm was a *harmless* / *terrifying* experience.
3 Make sure the bags are *secure* / *risky* before you set off.
4 This snake looks dangerous, but it's *harmless* / *injured* really.
5 I wouldn't ride a bike without a helmet. It's *secure* / *risky*.
6 Have you lost your phone again? You're so *careless* / *harmless*!

3 **Complete the sentences with your own ideas.**

1 The most terrifying experience I had was when ______________________ .
2 I injured my ______________________ when ______________________ .
3 I think ______________________ (sport) is risky because ______________________ .
4 The most secure place to keep valuable things is ______________________ .

THE GREAT *Penguin* RESCUE

In June of 2000, a ship called MV Treasure sank near Cape Town, South Africa, causing a massive oil spill. More than a thousand tons of oil went into the ocean, near an area where 75,000 penguins lived. Roughly 20,000 African penguins were covered with oil and as a result couldn't swim or even walk properly. It was very unlikely that they would survive, so a huge rescue operation was begun to save them. The operation, which lasted for 12 weeks, was only successful because of the 45,000 volunteers who offered their time and skills for free, in order to rescue the unfortunate birds.

It's an incredible story. At every stage, the rescuers faced enormous problems. First, the penguins had to be caught and transported 800 kilometers by air to a recovery center. They were then kept in a quiet place for several days so that they could get used to their new home. During this time and throughout the three months, the penguins had to be fed. As their diet is 98% fish, it isn't easy to find enough fish for 20,000 penguins – they need about ten tons a day! What's more, feeding them is dangerous, as they have extremely sharp beaks, and many volunteers got bitten.

Next, the oil had to be removed, and to do this, each one of the 20,000 birds was washed by hand. First, the oil had to be removed from their feathers by washing them in detergent, and then they had to be dried under special lamps. This was done repeatedly until there was no more oil on their bodies. The penguins then had to be put into pools to swim every day until their feathers had recovered completely.

When the penguins were completely clean and had recovered from their awful experience, they were returned to the wild. They were released into the wild in groups of several hundred at a time. Luckily, penguins are naturally good at finding their way home and it only took them two to three weeks to swim back to the place where they lived.

"The Great Penguin Rescue" was the world's biggest and most successful rescue of live animals. The animal experts and volunteers were the heroes of the rescue. Without them, the penguins would almost certainly not have survived. These people really cared about saving an endangered species.

Dyan deNapoli, who was one of the rescuers, wrote a book about the experience, *The Great Penguin Rescue*. At the time of the oil spill, she was working as a penguin expert at an aquarium in the US. As soon as she heard about the accident, she persuaded her boss to let her go to South Africa to help with the emergency. She knew that the entire species of African penguins was at risk and could become extinct. Her book tells the story of the dramatic rescue and her interest in penguins. The information about this type of seabird is interesting and helps readers to understand some of the problems involved in the rescue. Unsurprisingly, the author is now known as the "Penguin Lady"!

READING

1 What do numbers 1–6 refer to? Match them with letters a–f. Then read the article and check.

1 1,000+
2 75,000
3 20,000
4 12
5 45,000
6 10

a the number of penguins covered by the oil
b the number of tons of fish needed every day to feed the penguins
c the number of tons of oil that went into the ocean
d the number of weeks that were needed to save the penguins
e the number of penguins that lived in the area
f the number of people who helped to save the penguins

2 Read the article again. Answer the questions.

1 Why was the rescue necessary?
______
2 Why did the rescue operation work?
______
3 What were the two problems with feeding the penguins?
______
4 What made cleaning the penguins so difficult?
______
5 How did the penguins get back to their original home?
______
6 Why was Dyan deNapoli so interested in helping with the rescue?
______

3 CRITICAL THINKING Read the article again and complete the diagram with facts about penguins.

Penguins

1 food
______
______

2 body
______
______

3 abilities
______
______

4 status
______
______

DEVELOPING Writing

A story about a rescue

1 INPUT **Read the story. What lessons did Izzy learn?**

Don't go surfing

1 when you're ______________________.

2 when you're ______________________.

RESCUE STORY

1 Izzy and her friends had been surfing all day. The others had gone back to the campsite, but she wanted to go into the water one last time.

2 It was so hot that she hadn't worn her wetsuit all day, but now the water felt [1] cold ____________ . She tried to get on her surfboard, but there were such [2] strong ____________ waves that she was pushed under the water again and again. She soon felt [3] very tired ____________ . She started panicking. She tried shouting for help even though she couldn't see anyone nearby.

3 Rory had just gotten into the water when he heard Izzy's shouts. As he swam closer, he could see she was in danger. [4] Luckily ____________ for Izzy, Rory was a firefighter and knew what to do in an emergency. He managed to help her onto her surfboard, which he pulled along while he swam to shore. By this time, the lifeguard had arrived. Rory and the lifeguard thought Izzy was probably suffering from cold water shock, so they wrapped her in dry towels to keep her warm until the ambulance arrived.

4 Izzy soon recovered from her experience, but she now realizes how lucky she was that day. Rory had saved her life. If he hadn't reached her so [5] fast ____________ , she might have drowned.

She understands how [6] stupid ____________ it was to go into the water by herself, especially when she was tired because she had been surfing all day. "I've learned my lesson the hard way," she says.

2 ANALYZE **Adverbs and extreme adjectives help to make a story more exciting. Replace the underlined words in the story with the adverbs and extreme adjectives in the list.**

exhausted | fortunately | freezing
irresponsible | powerful | rapidly

3 **Short sentences can make a story sound more dramatic. Underline the short sentences in the story.**

4 **Match the content (a–d) with the paragraphs (1–4).**

Paragraph 1 ☐
Paragraph 2 ☐
Paragraph 3 ☐
Paragraph 4 ☐

a What happened
b The rescue
c Results/consequences
d Setting the scene

5 PLAN **Choose one of these sentences to begin a story about a rescue. Then make a plan for each of the paragraphs in Exercise 4.**

a The weather was perfect as we set off. What could possibly go wrong?
b It was a bad mistake to go there in the first place.
c "We were so lucky," is certainly true in this case.

6 PRODUCE **Write your story about a rescue (200–250 words). Use your plan from Exercise 5. Make sure you include all the points in the checklist.**

✓ CHECKLIST

Use some short sentences to add drama to your story.

Include some adjectives and adverbs to make your story exciting.

In the last paragraph, explain how the person felt after the rescue.

LISTENING

1 11.02 **Listen to the three dialogues. Match what the boy is doing with each dialogue (1–3). There is one extra option.**

a Saving someone ☐
b Helping someone ☐
c Trying to win a competition ☐
d Giving some news ☐

2 11.02 **Listen again and mark the sentences T (true) or F (false). Then correct the false sentences.**

1
a The girl doesn't mind being busy. ☐
b The boy offers to finish writing the article. ☐
2
a The boy isn't going out this weekend. ☐
b The girl decides to go to the music festival. ☐
3
a A friend of theirs helped to avoid a tragedy. ☐
b The girl doesn't think Danielle was very brave. ☐

3 11.02 **Listen again and complete the dialogues.**

1
A How do you find the time to do so much?
B I don't know. It just happens. I'm [1]________________ I don't know where to start!
A I just came to [2]________________ you were free, but I don't [3]________________ you. What can I do?

2
A How come?
B [4]________________ win first prize at the music festival.
A Well, I'd better buy a ticket for the music festival [5]________________ miss your winning performance!

3
A The wind was [6]________________ he lost control of the boat. He was [7]________________ crashing into the riverbank, but the boat hit a rock instead and he fell into the water.
B So, you mean Danielle [8]________________ from the river?
A Right. She's a strong swimmer and pulled the boy out of the water. Not only that, but she went back in [9]________________ the boat.

DIALOGUE

4 **Put the lines of the dialogues in order.**

1
☐ **A** Oh? Why not?
☐ **A** Where are you going?
☐ **A** Why on earth do you want a new one?
☐ **A** To get some things?
☐ **B** Into town.
☐ **B** To have the same one as everyone else, of course.
☐ **B** So as not to spend any money. I'm saving up for a new phone.
☐ **B** No, just window shopping today. I'm not going to buy anything.

2
☐ **A** A marathon? What on earth for?
☐ **A** Why's that?
☐ **A** Wow, that's not much food. Not hungry?
☐ **A** In shape? Are you going to start running or something?
☐ **B** No, I've just decided I want to eat less.
☐ **B** To lose weight and to get in shape.
☐ **B** So as to raise money for charity.
☐ **B** Actually, I've already started. I go to the gym, too. It's in order to run a marathon.

5 **Write two dialogues of four to six lines each.**

For each one:

- choose a person from the list below
- think of "why" questions to ask the person
- think of the person's answer(s).

Look back at Exercise 4 to help you.

Someone who wrote a book review
Someone who walked 30 kilometers in the snow
Someone who wants to be a firefighter
Someone who wants to work for a charity

____
____
____
____
____
____
____
____
____
____
____
____
____
____
____

READING AND USE OF ENGLISH

Gapped text

EXAM GUIDE

You will read a text from which six sentences have been removed. You have to complete the text by choosing from the sentences in the list. There is one extra sentence which you don't need to use.

- First, read through the text, ignoring the gaps, for general understanding.
- Pay particular attention to the sentences before and after each gap.
- Think about the type of information needed to fill the gap. Then look at the list of options and choose one.
- Try it in the gap and re-read the paragraph to make sure it makes sense.
- If the gap is the last sentence of a paragraph, read the first sentence of the next one.

1 **You are going to read about a girl who had a scary experience while on holiday. Six sentences have been removed from the text. Choose from the sentences A–G the one that fits each gap (1–6). There is one extra sentence which you do not need to use.**

Trapped!

Last year Ellie went on holiday to the French Alps with her parents and brother, Ethan. They are all keen mountain climbers and they were looking forward to five days of climbing. They weren't planning to get to any great height, but rather concentrate on a series of challenging smaller climbs.

The first day they tackled a 50-metre cliff face. It was a popular climb and there were several teams doing the same thing. It wasn't too difficult, and they all managed to reach the top within a couple of hours. 1_______ It was about 11 am and the sun was really starting to warm the rock face. They didn't feel like making the descent in the midday sun, so they decided to wait a few hours and explore the surroundings. Ellie and Ethan set off to investigate some nearby caves. They'd done a bit of caving before and these caves looked pretty exciting. They were deep and dark, but that didn't stop them. After about 10 metres the entrance tunnel became really narrow. Ellie warned her brother they'd better leave. 2_______ He could hear water and was sure there was an underground lake not far ahead. Ellie wasn't so sure, but before she knew it Ethan had squeezed through a narrow gap in the rocks. 3_______ Reluctantly, Ellie started pushing herself through the gap. She was scared. It was pitch black and she couldn't see a thing. She could feel the cold rock pushing against her chest. She was finding it hard to breathe. And then suddenly she was stuck. 4_______ She couldn't move forwards or backwards. She screamed out to Ethan. He could just reach her arm. He grabbed it and pulled and pulled but it was no good. She was going nowhere. Of course, he couldn't go and get help because she was blocking his way out.

For ten minutes they shouted and screamed but no one came. Ellie's body was sore and although the walls of the cave were cold, a hot sweat covered her body. She was beginning to feel dizzy. 5_______ The brother and sister began to feel sure they were going to die there.

After what must have been hours, they finally heard voices calling their names. Ellie was too weak to respond, but Ethan called back. Within seconds their parents were with them. Their dad tried pulling Ellie out. When she screamed out in pain, he realised that they needed professional help.

By the time the helicopter arrived more than two hours later, Ellie's body was freezing. 6_______ Ellie was hardly conscious when the rescue team finally reached her, but they knew exactly what to do. They sprayed the rock face and then slowly started to pull gently. Then with one last sudden pull, Ellie was free. She'd never felt so happy. Then, amazingly, a few seconds later, she was joined by her brother, who had just squeezed himself back through with no problem at all.

Ellie was taken by helicopter to hospital but released that evening. Apart from a few bad bruises, she was fine.

A Her parents were scared they were going to lose her.
B He wanted to continue.
C Ellie's leg was broken in two places.
D She tried to turn but it was no good.
E Ethan kept talking to keep her conscious.
F He called his sister to join him.
G The views were incredible.

12 LIFE'S FIRSTS

Grammar rap!

GRAMMAR
Phrasal verbs

→ SB p.112

1 ★☆☆ Put the words in order to make sentences. For the sentences that contain separable phrasal verbs, write both options.

1 Rachel / flowers / up / sent / to / cheer / We / her / some

____

2 quickly / came / after / Louis / operation / to / the

____

3 of / away / Maya / took / our / while / cat / care / we / were

____

4 excuses / makes / incredible / up / some / Leo

____

5 couldn't / traffic lights / was / out / so / we / foggy / make / the / It

____

6 moved / the / coast / Our / neighbors / to / away

____

7 I / gym / into / yesterday / Rex / at / ran / the

____

8 runners / are / many / part / in / the / taking / How / race

____

9 I / answer / can't / the / out / work

____

10 you / glasses / your / on / Can / put

____

2 ★★☆ Circle the correct phrasal verb and write it in the correct form. Some verbs are from Unit 7.

1 You'd better ________________ your jacket. It's cold. (put on / take up)

2 I haven't found my ticket yet, but I'm going to ________________ looking for it! (keep on / take care of)

3 Can you help me? I can't ________________ (work out / give up) the meaning of this sentence.

4 I often ________________ old friends from elementary school when I'm in town. (find out / run into)

5 Paula was really late – she only ________________ at ten o'clock. (end up / show up)

6 We've ________________ the invitation because we'll be on vacation then. (turn down / put on)

7 My dad has ________________ wind surfing. His first lesson was last Monday. (take up / take off)

8 Lily was feeling sad, but we managed to ________________ (cheer up / make out) by going for a walk in the park.

3 ★★☆ Circle the correct options.

1 We can't *make out* / *make it out* who the people in this photo are. Do you know?

2 Oh, so you're learning the guitar? When did you *take up it* / *take it up*?

3 Don't worry about sending me the information. I'll *find it out* / *find out it* myself.

4 Leroy started learning to dance but *gave up it* / *gave it up* after a few lessons.

5 My sister isn't well, but my mom's *taking her care of* / *taking care of her*.

6 We were going to fly, but when we *worked it out* / *worked out it*, the train was cheaper.

7 Where's your jacket? You'd better *put it on* / *put on it* because it's snowing outside!

4 ★★★ Complete the journal entry with a phrasal verb from the list in the correct form and, where necessary, a pronoun (*it, them, him, her,* etc.).

cheer up | end up | find out | give up
make up | move away | run into
set off | show up | work out

My friend Archie [1]________________ from our town a few months ago and he's feeling pretty sad. Last Friday, some friends and I planned a surprise visit to [2]________________. We [3]________________ an excuse and told Archie to be at the town square at 6 p.m.

We [4]________________ right after school. We missed the first bus because I was late, so we got the next one, but it was the wrong one and we [5]________________ at the bus station! We [6]________________ which bus we needed to catch and finally got to Archie's town at 6:10 p.m. We ran to the square, but Archie didn't [7]________________. Actually, he'd arrived at six, waited for ten minutes and then [8]________________. We were looking for a café when we [9]________________ Archie along the street! He thought the story of our adventure was really funny – especially when we [10]________________ we'd missed the last bus home! At least our visit was a success: Archie felt happier!

I wish / If only + past perfect

→ SB p.115

5 ★★☆ Circle the correct options.

Stefan went to his friend Taylor's party, but he didn't have a very good time. Here's what he thinks.

1 "I wish I *hadn't gone / didn't go* to the party."
2 "I wish Taylor *hadn't invited / didn't invite* me."
3 "If only *I knew / I'd known* about the awful music!"
4 "I wish they *accepted / had accepted* the offer of my playlist – but they said it was uncool!"
5 "If only *they'd played / they played* that Katy Perry song – then Kirsty would have danced with me."
6 "If only Kirsty *had danced / danced* with me! But Freddie was there."
7 "I wish Freddie *wasn't / hadn't been* there."
8 "And I wish I *hadn't worn / didn't wear* my yellow pants and red shirt."

6 ★★☆ **Read what Kirsty says and write sentences using *I wish* or *If only*.**

0 "Stefan didn't ask me to dance."
I wish Stefan had asked me to dance.
1 "Stefan wore yellow pants and a red shirt."
____
2 "They played awful music."
____
3 "Freddie wasn't in a good mood."
____
4 "Stefan ate so much food that he felt sick."
____
5 "Freddie laughed at Stefan."
____
6 "Stefan didn't enjoy himself."
____
7 "My parents picked me up at 11 p.m. I was the first to leave."
____
8 "I didn't have a good time."
____

7 ★★★ **Look at the pictures. For each person, write a sentence using *I wish* or *if only*.**

1 ____________________

3 ____________________

2 ____________________

4 ____________________

GET IT RIGHT!

Separable verbs

Learners often have problems with word order when using separable verbs.

✓ *I got an invitation, but I turned it down.*
✗ *I got an invitation, but I ~~turned down it~~.*

Choose the correct sentence in each pair. Sometimes both sentences are correct.

1 a I will pick you up at 7:30. ☐
b I will pick up you at 7:30. ☐
2 a When I left, I forgot to take out my memory stick. ☐
b When I left, I forgot to take my memory stick out. ☐
3 a I looked for her number on my phone. ☐
b I looked her number for on my phone. ☐
4 a I tried to solve the puzzle but I couldn't work out it. ☐
b I tried to solve the puzzle but I couldn't work it out. ☐
5 a I would like to get back my money for that trip. ☐
b I would like to get my money back for that trip. ☐
6 a You should think over it. ☐
b You should think it over. ☐
7 a The man gave me my bag back. ☐
b The man gave me back my bag. ☐

VOCABULARY

Phrasal verbs (2)

→ SB p.112

1 ★★☆ **Complete the sentences with the correct preposition.**

1 "What's the matter with you?" "Everything!" "Cheer ____________ . It can't be that bad!"

2 We really missed our neighbors when they moved ____________ .

3 They ran ____________ some old friends that they hadn't seen for years.

4 How much have we spent today? Let's work it ____________ .

5 When the ball hit Matt on the head, he collapsed, but he soon came ____________ .

6 I'd put your boots ____________ if I were you. It's very wet.

7 They look so much like each other – I can never work ____________ who is who!

8 Are you taking part ____________ the art competition?

9 I can't come out tonight, I'm taking ____________ my younger brother.

10 I forgot my glasses. I can't make ____________ what's written here.

2 ★★★ **Complete the dialogues with the correct form of the phrasal verbs in Exercise 1.**

1

A Hey, Lucie. [1]________________ ! What's the matter?

B I'm visiting the university next week, but I'm a bit worried about the trip. I've never been on a train by myself.

A I went there last year. The journey is really easy.

B I looked at the website, but it's really confusing and I can't [2]________________ what I have to do.

A No problem! I'll help you [3]________________ which trains to catch.

B Thanks.

2

A Hey, I [4]________________ Jonathan the other day. Have you heard his family is [5]________________ ? They're moving to California.

B California? Lucky them! But I'll miss Jonathan. He always [6]________________ in the school swimming competition. I might have a chance of winning now!

3

A Oliver? Could you come straight home?

B Uh, OK, Mom. Is there a problem?

A I have to go out in ten minutes and there's no one here to [7]________________ Chloe.

B No problem. I'm [8]________________ my jacket and I'll be back in five minutes.

Nervousness and fear

→ SB p.115

3 ★★☆ **Complete the crossword.**

1 Some people do this if they are very hot or very nervous.

2 If you're frightened, you shouldn't do this. Stay calm.

3 Sometimes people bite these when they are nervous.

4 We often do this when we are very cold or very nervous.

5 extremely scared

6 Some people do this hard when they are tired or afraid.

7 People sometimes do this when they are afraid or nervous.

8 Sometimes this gets dry if you are nervous.

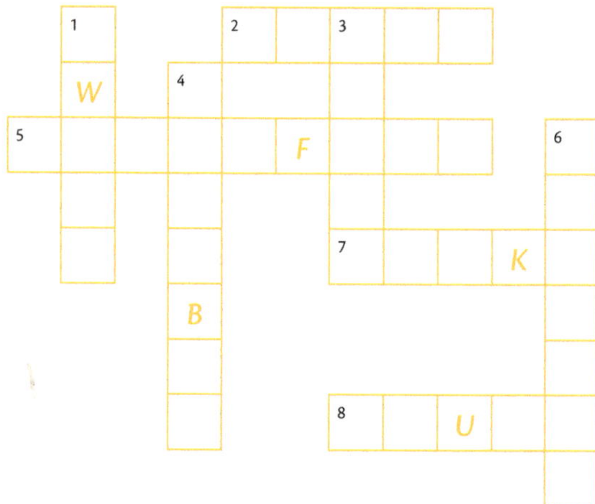

PRONUNCIATION

Different pronunciations of *ea*

Go to page 121.

4 ★★★ **Complete the words in the story.**

When I arrived for my interview, I was a little nervous. They showed me to a waiting room – there were three other people there. One man looked terrible – he was [1]b____________ his n____________ and walking up and down the room. He was walking slowly, but even so, he was [2]b____________ h____________ . The woman was [3]s____________ so much that she had to keep wiping her face. And the other guy looked very scared, [4]t____________ in fact! He was [5]t____________ all the time and talking to himself very quietly.

I sat down and tried to relax, but it wasn't easy with those people around me. I looked at my hands – they were [6]s____________ a little, so I took some deep breaths to calm down. "Don't [7]p____________ ," I said to myself. "It'll be OK."

When I finally went in and they asked me a question, my [8]m____________ got completely d____________ and I could hardly talk. I thought the interview had gone really badly. But in the end, I got the job!

REFERENCE

Nervousness and fear

- to tremble
- (your) mouth goes dry
- to bite your nails
- to breathe hard
- to panic
- to shake
- to sweat
- (to be) terrified

PHRASAL VERBS (2)

cheer up	make up	move away	run into	take care of
come to	make out	put on	take part in	work out

VOCABULARY *EXTRA*

1 **Match the phrasal verbs (1–5) with the phrases (a–e). Look at the pictures and sentences in Exercise 2 to help you.**

1 break down ☐
2 carry out ☐
3 look into ☐
4 sort out ☐
5 stand out ☐

a do something, e.g., research or experiments
b organize something that is messy or complicated
c a machine stops working
d be different from others in some way
e examine the facts

2 **Complete the sentences with the correct form of the phrasal verbs in Exercise 1.**

1 New cars shouldn't ________________, but ours did!

2 Mom's ________________ our vacation: a train trip around Europe!

3 They ________________ experiments to find new medicines in this lab.

4 Kelly ________________ from the other kids in this photo. She's wearing rain boots!

5 The police are ________________ the burglary.

3 **Answer the questions with your own ideas.**

1 I'd like scientists to carry out research into ______________________.
2 I need to sort out ______________________.
3 ______________________ is a singer/actor who stands out from the others because ______________________.
4 I'll never forget the time the ______________________ broke down because ______________________.
5 I think our principal needs to look into ______________________ because ______________________.

IMPORTANT FIRSTS FOR BLACK AMERICANS

In 2008, Barack Obama became the Black president of the United States. This was another victory in a long history of firsts for people of color in the US. Here are two more that you may not know about.

1 JACKIE ROBINSON:

the first Black player in Major League Baseball (MLB)

Jackie Robinson became an American sporting legend despite a difficult start in life. His family had very little money, but Jackie had plenty of talent and ambition. He was interested in sports from an early age and took up a variety of different sports at school and college. At the age of 26, he decided to concentrate on baseball when he joined his first professional team.

In 1947, Jackie Robinson ran onto the field to play for the Brooklyn Dodgers in New York. Some players, both on the other team and on his own team, weren't happy about playing with him. However, the numbers of Black fans at Dodgers' games started going up. Robinson played baseball exceptionally well, even though he was treated badly for many years by all kinds of people – other players, coaches, and fans.

Jackie Robinson was chosen as the best player in the MLB in 1949, and then, in 1962, he became a member of the Baseball Hall of Fame. He was, of course, the first Black player to do so. These weren't his only firsts. He was the first Black baseball reporter on TV and became the first Black vice-president of a major American company.

Jackie Robinson died in 1972, but he is still remembered. In 1992, the MLB announced that no other player would ever wear the number 42, his jersey number. Since then, the date he took part in his first MLB game has been celebrated as Jackie Robinson Day.

2 OPRAH WINFREY:

the first Black woman to host a TV show in the US

Oprah Winfrey had a hard life as a child. At the age of six, she moved away from her grandmother and went to live with her mother, but she didn't stay there long because they didn't get along. She ended up with her father, who changed the direction of her life by encouraging her to work hard at school. At the age of 19, while she was still a student, she got her first job in television.

In 1984, Oprah Winfrey became the first Black woman to host a TV show in the US. *The Oprah Winfrey Show*, which ended in 2011, was one of the most well-known TV shows in the world. It included interviews with famous people as well as educational features, such as self-improvement ideas and a book club. This was so popular that the books she chose nearly always became bestsellers.

She has appeared in several movies, including *The Color Purple*. In April of 2000, she launched *O* magazine, which became one of the most successful magazines ever. In 2003, *Forbes* magazine listed her as the first Black woman to become a billionaire. *Time* magazine has included Oprah in their list of the 100 Most Influential People in the World several times.

Although she is one of the highest-paid celebrities ever, she's still busy working on movies, television, and writing. She also continues to promote education for women and children and has run national safety campaigns on issues such as encouraging people not to use their phones while driving.

READING

1 **Read the article and answer the question.**

What were Jackie Robinson's and Oprah Winfrey's lives like when they were children?

____

2 **Read the article again. Mark the sentences T (true) or F (false). Then correct the false sentences.**

1 Jackie Robinson only played basketball in college. ☐
2 Only players on the other team didn't want Jackie Robinson to play in Major League Baseball. ☐
3 Many people behaved badly towards Robinson. ☐
4 MLB players are proud to wear the number 42 shirt. ☐
5 Oprah Winfrey's father believed education was important. ☐
6 *The Oprah Winfrey Show* was her first job in TV. ☐
7 She works as a teacher for women and children. ☐

3 CRITICAL THINKING **Read the two articles again and find similarities and differences between Jackie Robinson and Oprah Winfrey. Think about their backgrounds, education, careers, and achievements.**

A Similarities:

____
____
____
____

B Differences:

____
____
____
____

DEVELOPING Writing

A blog entry about a mistake

1 INPUT **Read the blog entry. What was the result of the writer's mistake?**

____

A BIG mistake

If only I'd stopped to think! That's what I say when I look back at that big mistake. I was 12 and I'd started to play tennis. I couldn't get enough of it. When there was no one to play with, I used to hit tennis balls against a wall. And the best wall was at my school, not far from my house. It was about six meters high. Perfect!

There was a hole in the fence around the school so sometimes I crawled through it, into the schoolyard to hit tennis balls against that wall. I wasn't supposed to be there after school hours, but I didn't care.

One evening I hit my only ball onto the roof. There it was. Stuck. Now what was I going to do? I had to get it down again. There was a drainpipe on the wall, going up to the roof – I didn't think, I just started to climb. Was I crazy? Absolutely! And what happened? The pipe broke, of course, and I fell.

I could have been killed. Luckily someone saw what happened and called an ambulance. I'd broken my right leg. The doctors did their best, but it never mended properly. My parents were furious because I'd done such a dangerous thing. The school was angry because I shouldn't have been there. I was unhappy because I was in the hospital.

I wish I'd stopped to think! But I was only 12, after all.

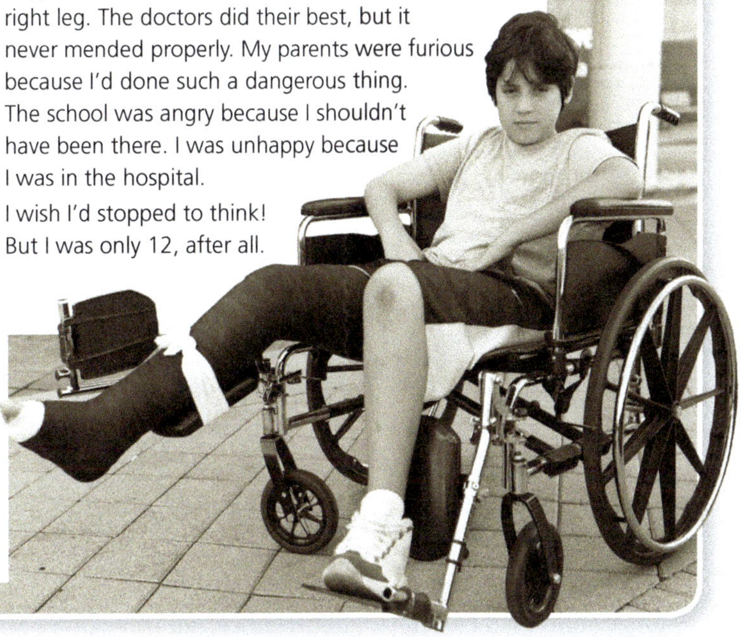

2 ANALYZE **Underline three questions that the writer asks.**

1 Are they really questions for the reader?

____

2 What effect does the writer want to create by using them?

____

3 **Underline three single word sentences in the text. Why does the writer do this? Choose the correct answer.**

A to avoid problems with grammar
B to create more impact
C to use fewer words

4 **Rewrite the underlined parts. Use either a short question or a single word. There are several possible answers.**

1 I told him the news. This was a mistake!

____

2 He got really angry and started shouting. I didn't know why he was shouting at me.

____

3 There was clearly a problem. I didn't know what it was.

____

4 Then he walked out and closed the door. He closed it loudly.

____

5 PLAN **You are going to write a story about a mistake you or someone else made. It can be real or imaginary. Include one of these sentences in your story. Then write a plan with your ideas, using the paragraph guide below.**

A I wish I hadn't said it.
B If only I'd known that I was breaking the rules.
C I wish he / she / they had told me.

- First paragraph: Describe the scene / situation
- Middle paragraphs: Tell the story of what happened
- Last paragraph: Explain the result / consequences

6 PRODUCE **Write your story (200 words). Use your plan from Exercise 5. Make sure you include all the points in the checklist.**

CHECKLIST

Use an informal style.
Include some one-word sentences.
Ask questions for dramatic effect.
Use phrases that express regret.

LISTENING

1 12.02 **Listen to two conversations. Answer the questions.**

1 What does Jamie regret?

___

2 Why is Duncan annoyed with Chiara?

___

2 12.02 **Listen again. Answer the questions.**

1

a How much did Jamie pay?

___

b Why does Anna know so much about buying a smart speaker online?

___

c What does Anna regret at the end?

___

2

a What is the secret that Chiara tells Duncan?

___

b Why does Chiara think it's OK to tell him the secret?

___

c Why is it a problem that Chiara has told Sam the secret?

___

3 **Complete the dialogues with the correct form of the verbs in the list.**

do | keep | know | say | tell (x2)

1

Jamie No, I didn't know that. But I wish I ___ last week!

2

Jamie If only I ___ a bit of research to find out!

3

Anna Now I wish I ___ you about it!

4

Chiara Did you know his dad had been in prison?

Duncan No, I didn't, and I wish you ___ me.

5

Chiara Well, I wish you ___ something.

6

Duncan Sam can't keep a secret and you know it. Oh, if only you ___ quiet!

DIALOGUE

4 **Put the lines in order to make three short dialogues.**

1

Scott Oh Bridget, if only you'd been on time.

Bridget ___

Scott ___

Bridget ___

Scott ___

2

Raul I wish we hadn't come to this restaurant.

Frances ___

Raul ___

Frances ___

Raul ___

3

Joanne My parents are furious with me.

Sean ___

Joanne ___

Sean ___

Joanne ___

1 And it's such a shame. The show was amazing.
2 What? Bad reviews? If only you'd told me that before. We could have gone somewhere else.
3 I know. But it wasn't my fault. It was the traffic.
4 I know! If only I'd left when Zac and Sally did – then I wouldn't be in all this trouble.
5 Yes, exactly. I wish I hadn't gone to that party. I didn't even enjoy it.
6 But we came here because you said you wanted to eat Indian food.
7 I wish I had left earlier. But that's history. I missed the show.
8 I'm not surprised. I found a lot of bad reviews online about the food here.
9 Well, if you didn't enjoy it, why didn't you leave earlier? You're crazy.
10 There's always traffic. Why didn't you leave home earlier?
11 Why's that? Is it because you were out late on Saturday?
12 I know, and usually I love Indian food, but this is awful!

5 **Choose one of the lines below and use it to start or end a five-line dialogue.**

I wish I hadn't come.
I wish I'd never bought it.
If only I hadn't eaten so much.
If only I'd checked online.

TOWARDS B2 First for Schools

READING AND USE OF ENGLISH

Gapped text

1 **You are going to read another extract from *Bullring Kid and Country Cowboy*. Six sentences have been removed from the text. Choose from the sentences A–G the one that fits each gap (1–6). There is one extra sentence that you do not need to use. Look back at the exam guide in Unit 11 on how to answer this question type.**

Fletcher and Fizza climbed quietly down the hill a few more metres and looked out carefully from behind a small bush. Cloudy's kidnapper was talking to another man who he had met on the beach. [1]______ In the dark they could see that one of them was fat and the other one was thin. It was the thin one that had stolen Cloudy.

'Well done! That looks like a nice horse!' the fat man said.

'Yes, we should get a good price for it,' replied the thin man. 'When's the boat going to get here?'

'Any moment now … I'll get the others,' said the fat man.

He disappeared behind some big rocks in a corner of the beach. After a few seconds, he came back out of the dark. [2]______ 'They're our horses!' whispered Fletcher angrily. 'Those men have been keeping them here!'

The men were obviously waiting for a boat that would get them off the island. A few moments later a green light flashed three times out at sea.

'Hey! That's the sign! They're here!' the thin man shouted.

Fizza and Fletcher realised that if they were going to stop these men, they had to act now before help arrived.

'OK, Fizza,' whispered Fletcher, 'this is what we've got to do …'.

Seconds later, Fizza waited in her position while Fletcher gave a low whistle. All three horses on the sand put their heads up and listened, but the men didn't notice anything. [3]______ Then Fletcher whistled again and the horses began to jump in excitement. This did surprise the men. Every time Fletcher whistled, the horses jumped until they had managed to pull their ropes free from the men's hands. They began to run in circles around them.

'Catch them, stupid!' shouted one of the men.

'You try! They're too quick!' replied the other one.

[4]______ She ran onto the beach, jumped in the air, gave a high kick and knocked the fat man down to the ground.

'Oi!' shouted the thin man. He tried to run and help his friend, but all three horses moved into his way. [5]______ Fizza sat on top of the fat man, who lay face down, and held his arms behind his back.

'Ow! That hurts!' he cried.

'Well, don't move then!' replied Fizza.

She watched as Fletcher tied the thin man's hands and feet together with a rope and then she looked out to sea. [6]______ 'What are we going to do when that boat gets here?' she asked Fletcher.

'Yeah!' said the fat man through a mouthful of sand. 'What are you going to do?

A He was leading two large horses.
B He couldn't move!
C They were too busy looking for their boat.
D He had three other men with him.
E The lights from the kidnappers' boat were getting much nearer, making the horses run away.
F The men were so close that Fizza and Fletcher could hear them speak.
G This was the moment that Fizza was waiting for.

CONSOLIDATION

LISTENING

1 12.03 **Listen to Billy talking about the first time he went surfing. Answer the questions.**

1 How old was he?

____

2 How long was he in the water for before he went out to the big waves?

____

3 What did he do when he realized he was alone in the water?

____

4 Who rescued him?

____

2 12.03 **Complete the sentences about Billy with the words in the list. Then listen again and check.**

confident | embarrassed | excited
relieved | scared | worried

Billy felt …

1 _______________ when his cousins offered to take him surfing.
2 _______________ after half an hour in the shallow water.
3 _______________ after a few minutes in the deep water.
4 _______________ after the big wave hit him.
5 _______________ when he saw the lifeguard approaching.
6 _______________ when he got back to the beach afterwards.

VOCABULARY

3 **Complete the second sentences with negative prefixes.**

1 It isn't possible.
It's _______________ .
2 He isn't very patient.
He's quite _______________ .
3 The party isn't formal.
It's an _______________ .
4 I expect you to be more responsible.
I don't expect you to be so _______________ .
5 This sofa isn't very comfortable.
It's a very _______________ .
6 I'm not sure what you're doing is legal.
I think what you're doing is _______________ .

4 **Match the parts of the sentences.**

1 The doctors did everything they could to save ☐
2 He's still in the hospital, but the doctors say he's ☐
3 That house is very old. It's in ☐
4 When I get nervous, I can't stop ☐
5 Does your mouth go ☐
6 He got on the wrong train ☐
7 We're moving ☐
8 Come on! Cheer ☐
9 Lena's looking ☐

a danger of falling down.
b and ended up in Chicago.
c away because Dad's got a new job.
d up. Your grades aren't that bad!
e out of danger now.
f after her little sister this afternoon.
g dry when you're scared?
h her life after the accident.
i biting my nails.

GRAMMAR

5 **Complete the sentences with the correct form of the verbs in parentheses.**

1 I don't have any money for the bus. I wish I _______________ all my money. (not spend)
2 So you don't really enjoy _______________ , you just do it for exercise? (swim)
3 Dad offered _______________ us a ride to the party. (give)
4 They've just bought a new car, so they can't afford _______________ on a trip this year. (go)
5 If only we _______________ more for breakfast. We're really hungry. (eat)
6 We moved to the city last year and I really miss _______________ in the countryside. (live)
7 Lisa doesn't mind _______________ you. She isn't busy. (help)
8 He wishes he _______________ his homework last night. There's no time to do it now. (do)
9 Don't worry about the problem. I'm sure we can _______________ . (work out / it)

DIALOGUE

6 🔊 12.04 **Put the dialogue in order. Then listen and check.**

- [ ] **Assistant** No, no, don't tell me. And keep the keypad covered up with your other hand.
- [ ] **Assistant** Here, let me help you. Put the card in like this and now enter your password.
- [ ] **Assistant** You have your card in the wrong way.
- [1] **Assistant** Is this your first time using the ATM?
- [ ] **Assistant** Well, that's what I'm here for, in order to help our customers.
- [ ] **Assistant** So as to keep it secret. You don't want other people seeing your password.
- [ ] **Man** OK, five, four …
- [ ] **Man** That's so embarrassing.
- [ ] **Man** Of course I don't. You're such a kind young man to help me.
- [ ] **Man** Yes, it is. How did you guess?
- [ ] **Man** Why do I need to do that?
- [ ] **Man** In that case, could you help me with my shopping at the supermarket, too?

READING

7 **Read the article. Circle the correct options.**

IF YOU DON'T SUCCEED AT FIRST, TRY, TRY AGAIN!

This proverb tells us never to give up on things that go wrong the first time. It must be true because there are plenty of people that kept on trying and ended up famous.

Bill Gates dropped out of college and then started a business, which failed. This was before starting Microsoft and inventing Windows – the most popular operating system in the world.

Disney is a global brand today, but Walt Disney didn't have an easy start. Once he lost his job because his boss thought he didn't have any imagination or good ideas! He tried a number of businesses that failed before discovering the secret for success – a little mouse named Mickey.

Who hasn't read *The Cat in the Hat* and the *Harry Potter* series? Well, we might not have had the chance to enjoy them if their authors had listened to all the publishers who refused to print them. Luckily, both Dr. Seuss and J. K. Rowling didn't give up until they found publishers that recognized their talents.

Vincent van Gogh, the Dutch artist whose paintings sell for millions of dollars these days, only managed to sell one painting in his lifetime. His lack of success didn't stop him from trying though. When he died, he left over 800 completed pictures.

And what about those great scientists? Surely, an intelligent person like Albert Einstein couldn't fail! He was a genius, wasn't he? Well, he was made to leave one school and refused entry to another, but he ended up winning a Nobel Prize for Physics. Then there was Charles Darwin. His father thought he was lazy and uninterested in school. He'd probably be very surprised to find out that Charles' work still influences scientists today.

So, the next time you feel like giving up, stop and think again – you might be a winner one day!

1 The writer *agrees* / *disagrees* with the proverb in the title.
2 Bill Gates *had* / *didn't have* the opportunity to study for a degree.
3 One of Walt Disney's employers suggested that he was *uncreative* / *impolite*.
4 Dr. Seuss and J. K. Rowling *offered* / *refused* to sell their books to many publishers.
5 Van Gogh decided to *keep on* / *give up* painting when he couldn't sell many pictures.
6 Einstein and Darwin were both *unsuccessful* / *irresponsible* at school.

WRITING

8 **Write a short text (150–200 words) about the first time you did something difficult (for example, rode a bike, went swimming in the ocean, cooked a meal, or spoke English to a native speaker). Include this information:**

- What it was
- How you felt before
- Any problems you had doing it
- How you felt when it was finished.

PRONUNCIATION

UNIT 7

Intonation – inviting, accepting, and refusing invitations

1 7.02 **Listen to the dialogues. For each one, decide if the speaker is accepting or refusing the invitation and check (✓) the correct box.**

0 Would you like to come with us to see a movie on Saturday?
Accepting ☑ Refusing ☐

1 Would you like to work on the history project with me?
Accepting ☐ Refusing ☐

2 Those bags look heavy. Can I help you carry them?
Accepting ☐ Refusing ☐

3 I'm going to ride my bike to the river and go for a swim. Do you want to come?
Accepting ☐ Refusing ☐

4 Didn't you bring anything to eat? Would you like half of my cheese sandwich?
Accepting ☐ Refusing ☐

5 I'm having some friends over for dinner next Saturday. Why don't you join us?
Accepting ☐ Refusing ☐

2 7.03 **Look at these extracts from the dialogues. For each one, is the speaker accepting (A) or refusing (R) the invitation? Listen to the extracts to check your answers.**

1 I'd love to come! ☐
2 I'm sorry, Pete. ☐
3 That's very kind of you. ☐
4 That's a great idea. ☐
5 Oh, thank you! ☐
6 What a shame. ☐

3 **Underline the stressed words in each of the sentences in Exercise 2 and circle the correct word to complete the rule.**

Intonation goes *up* / *down* when accepting an invitation.
Intonation goes *up* / *down* when refusing an invitation.

4 7.03 **Listen, check, and repeat.**

UNIT 8

Intonation – expressing surprise

1 8.03 **Read and listen to the dialogue, ignoring the spaces, and answer this question. Why didn't Harriet hold the ladder?**

ambulance | arm | ~~believe~~ | bookstore
cell | crash | English | highest
ladder (x2) | later | Tell | that | way

Anna You're not going to [0] *believe* this, but…
Ben [1] __________ me.
Anna Well, Harriet was at the [2] __________ yesterday and she asked the sales assistant for the new [3] __________ course book. It was on the [4] __________ shelf in the store!
Ben Right.
Anna So, the assistant had to get it down using a [5] __________. The next thing she knew, he'd fallen and broken his [6] __________!
Ben No! How did [7] __________ happen?
Anna He asked Harriet to hold the [8] __________, but she thought he told her to come back [9] __________. As she was leaving, she heard this terrible [10] __________!
Ben Really?
Anna Yes! At least she had her [11] __________ with her. She had to call for an [12] __________!
Ben No [13] __________!

2 8.03 **Complete the spaces. Listen again and check.**

3 8.04 **Ben changes his intonation to express surprise. Listen again, try to notice this, and repeat.**

UNIT 9

Moving word stress

1 9.01 **Listen and circle the stressed syllable.**

0 con•(grat)•u•late (v) — con•grat•u•(la)•tions (n)
1 nav•i•gate (v) — nav•i•ga•tion (n)
2 mys•ter•y (n) — mys•te•ri•ous (adj)
3 ar•tist (n) — ar•tis•tic (adj)
4 pre•sent (v) — pre•sent (n)
5 pho•to•graph (n) — pho•to•graph•y (n)
6 ex•plain (v) — ex•pla•na•tion (n)
7 in•ves•ti•gate (v) — in•ves•ti•ga•tion (n)
8 e•lec•tric (adj) — e•lec•tri•ci•ty (n)
9 mu•sic (n) — mu•si•cian (n)

2 9.01 **Listen again, check, and repeat.**

3 **Write the names of the people who do these jobs. Use a dictionary to help you.**

0 art _art•ist_
1 music ____________
2 navigation ____________
3 present (v) ____________
4 investigate ____________
5 electric ____________
6 research (v) ____________

4 9.02 **Listen, check, and repeat. Circle the stressed syllable in each of the jobs.**

UNIT 10

Short and long vowel sounds: /ɪ/ – /iː/ and /ɑ/ – /oʊ/

1 10.02 **Listen and circle the word you hear.**

0 ship – sheep
1 sit – seat
2 slip – sleep
3 chip – cheap
4 will – wheel
5 not – note
6 hop – hope
7 clock – cloak
8 want – won't
9 sock – soak

2 **Choose one word from each pair in Exercise 1 to complete the sentences.**

0 My room's such a mess that I can't find my other ___sock___!
1 Oh my goodness! Look at the ____________ – it's time to go home.
2 Look at the front ____________ . We have a flat tire!
3 We're going to the beach and I ____________ you can come with us.
4 Her grandparents are ____________ farmers.
5 Please ____________ down. The doctor will see you in a moment.
6 Danny ____________ go to the movies with us if we decide to see a horror movie.
7 I love my new sweater. And it was ____________ , too.
8 It's important to get about eight hours' ____________ a night.
9 Please make a ____________ in your planners that we don't have a class on Monday.

3 10.03 **Listen, check, and repeat.**

UNIT 11

Strong and weak forms: /tuː/ and /tə/

1 **Match the questions and answers.**

0 Do you think it's easy **to** make friends when you move **to** a new place? _d_
1 If it was up **to** you, would you go **to** a hot or cold place for your vacation? ☐
2 Would you star in a movie if you were asked **to**? ☐
3 Before coming **to** class, who was the last person you talked **to**? ☐
4 Which person, living or dead, do you most look up **to**? ☐
5 What kind of book would you write, if you had **to**? ☐

a I'd go **to** the mountains – it would be great **to** go skiing this winter!
b I talked **to** my mom on my cell phone – she wanted **to** know if I was coming home for lunch.
c Maybe my grandma – she's so kind and fun **to** be with.
d It depends on the place you move **to**. I think it's easier if you go **to** a large town or city.
e I don't think so – I don't even like going **to** the movies.
f Historical fiction, I think. I often think about what it would be like **to** live in the past.

2 11.01 **Listen and check your answers.**

3 **Underline the weak forms and circle the strong forms of *to* in the sentences in Exercise 1.**

4 11.01 **Listen again and check your answers.**

UNIT 12

Different pronunciations of *ea*

1 **Write the words in the correct columns.**

~~bread~~ | break | breakfast | breathe | clean
early | easy | healthy | heard | please
research | speak | steak | sweating | wear

1 /iː/ eat	2 /e/ head	3 /ɜr/ learn	4 /eɪ/ great	5 /ər/ bear
	bread			

2 12.01 **Listen, check, and repeat.**

GRAMMAR REFERENCE

UNIT 7

make / let and *be allowed to*

1 **We use *make (someone do)* to talk about forcing someone to do something that perhaps they don't want to do.**

*Our school **makes us wear** a uniform. (= We cannot choose; it's an obligation that our school gives us.)*
*My sister **made me clean** her bike. (= I could not choose; my sister forced me.)*

2 **We use *let (someone do)* to talk about permission to do the things we want to do.**

*Our parents **let us sleep** late on Sundays. (= Our parents give us permission to sleep late.)*
*I **let my brother use** my laptop on the weekend. (= I gave my brother permission to use my laptop.)*

3 **We use *(not) be allowed to (do something)* to say that someone has (or does not) have permission.**

***Are** we **allowed to use** our cell phones in here?*
*When my parents were children, they **weren't allowed to go** out at night.*

be / get used to

1 **To say that we are (not) accustomed to or (not) comfortable with doing certain things, we can use the expressions *be used to* and *get used to*.**

2 ***Be used to* refers to a state.**

*She**'s not used to eating** dinner so late.*

3 ***Get used to* refers to the change from something we weren't used to, to a situation that we are used to now.**

*It took her a long time to **get used to wearing** glasses.*

4 **These expressions are followed by a noun or noun phrase or the gerund (*-ing*) form of a verb.**

*The animals are not used to **people touching them**.*
*I'm getting used to **speaking** in public now.*

UNIT 8

Reported speech (review)

We use reported speech to report what someone said in the past. In reported speech, we often have to change the verb that was used in direct speech.

"It's ten o'clock," she said. ➜ *She said it **was** ten o'clock.*
*"It's **raining**," my mom said.* ➜ *My mom said it **was raining**.*
*"I**'ve had** a really bad day," he said.* ➜ *He said he**'d had** a really bad day.*
*"He **didn't remember** to call me," I said.* ➜ *I said he **hadn't remembered** to call me.*
*"I **can't do** this exercise," my friend said.* ➜ *My friend said she **couldn't do** the exercise.*
*"I**'ll pick** you up at eight," she said.* ➜ *She said she **would pick** me up at eight.*
*"We**'re going** to tell the police," she said.* ➜ *She said they **were going** to tell the police.*

But sometimes the tense doesn't change.

*"They**'d stolen** my car," she said.* ➜ *She said they**'d stolen** her car.*
*"No one **would** want it to happen," he said.* ➜ *He said that no one **would** want it to happen.*

Reported questions, requests, and imperatives

1 **With reported questions, we use statement word order and NOT question word order. We also do not use a question mark.**

*She asked me **who my friends were**.*
(NOT *They asked me ~~who were my friends?~~*)
*I asked her **what she did**.*
(NOT *I asked her ~~what did she do?~~*)
*They asked me **why I wanted the job**.*
(NOT *They asked me ~~why did I want the job?~~*)

2 **When we report yes / no questions, we use *if* (or *whether*) and statement word order.**

"Is that book good?"
➜ *She asked me **if the book was** good.*
"Do you eat fish?"
➜ *He asked me **whether I ate fish**.*

3 **When we report *wh-* questions (with *who* / *where* / *what* / *how* / *when*, etc.), we use the same question word and statement word order.**

"What are you looking at?"
➜ *He asked me **what I was looking at**.*
"Why did you leave the door open?"
➜ *They asked me **why I had left the door open**.*
"How much money did they steal?"
➜ *They asked me **how much money they'd stolen**.*

4 **With requests, we use *asked* + person + *to* (*do*).**

"Please help me with this, Mom."
➜ *He **asked his mom to help** him.*
"Can you close the door, please?"
➜ *She **asked me to close** the door.*

5 **With imperatives, we use *told* + person + (*not*) *to* (*do*).**

"Go away!"
➜ *He told me to go away.*
"Don't call the police!"
➜ *They told me not to call the police.*

UNIT 9

Modals of deduction (present)

Sometimes we express an opinion about whether something is true or not in the present, based on what we know or can see. We use the modal verbs *must* / *can't* / *might* / *could*.

1 **When we're sure that something is true, we often use *must* + verb.**

*They live in a really big house – they **must have** a lot of money.*

2 **When we're sure that something isn't true, we often use *can't* + verb.**

*That tomato is two weeks old, so it **can't be** good any more.*

3 **When we aren't sure, we often use *might* or *could* + verb, to show our uncertainty.**

*They're speaking Portuguese, so they **might be** Brazilian.*
*Maybe we shouldn't go in there – it **could be** dangerous.*

Modal verbs of deduction (past)

Sometimes we express an opinion about a past situation or event, based on what we know or can see in the present. We use the modal verbs *must* / *can't* / *might* / *could* + *have* + past participle.

*The wind blew this tree down. It **must have been** a really strong wind.*
*The door lock isn't broken, so the thieves **can't have gotten in** that way.*
*I'm not sure when my bike was stolen, but it **might have been** yesterday afternoon.*
*Police think that the criminals **could have taken** more than a million dollars.*

should(n't) have

We use *should* / *shouldn't have* (*done*) to criticize things that we, or other people, did in the past.

*You **should have come** to the party. (= You <u>didn't</u> come to the party, and I think that was a mistake.)*
*They **should have won**. (= They <u>didn't</u> win, and I think that was bad / wrong.)*
*You **shouldn't have taken** it without asking me. (= You <u>did</u> take it without asking me, and that was wrong.)*
*I **shouldn't have said** that. (= I <u>did</u> say it, and I think that I was wrong to do so.)*

UNIT 10

Future continuous

We use the future continuous to talk about things that will be in progress at a specified time in the future. The future continuous is formed by *will* + *be* + the *-ing* form of the verb.

*This time next week, **I'll be sitting** on a beach in Italy.*
*Twenty years from now, we **won't be using** money to buy things any more.*

Future perfect

If we want to talk about an action that will have been completed at a specified time in the future, we use the future perfect tense. The future perfect tense is formed by *will* + the present perfect.

*Some people think that by 2050, credit cards **will have disappeared**.*
*By Saturday, **I'll have spent** all my money – so I won't be able to go out on Sunday.*

UNIT 11

Verbs followed by gerund or infinitive

Some verbs in English are followed by *to* + infinitive; some are followed by a gerund (the *-ing* form of a verb).

1 **Some common verbs followed by *to* + infinitive are: *afford, choose, decide, expect, hope, learn, offer, promise, want.***

*The show's too expensive – I can't **afford to go**.*
*The other player's really good, so I don't **expect to win** the game.*
*You need to **learn to control** yourself and not get so angry.*
*I **promise to be** there on time.*

2 **Some common verbs followed by a gerund are: *avoid, enjoy, feel like, finish, imagine, (don't) mind, miss, practice, suggest.***

*That park's a little dangerous, so we **avoid going** there.*
*I don't want to work any more – I **feel like doing** something to enjoy myself.*
*I can't **imagine living** in a foreign country.*
*Do you ever **miss seeing** your friends when you travel?*

to / in order to / so as to

1 **When we want to give the reason why someone did something (the purpose), we can use *to* + infinitive. We can also use *in order to* or *so as to* – these are more formal.**

*I called her **to ask** about her about her trip.*
*It is important to arrive early **in order to save** time.*
*Please fill out this form **so as to help** us provide the best service for you.*

2 **When we want to make *in order to* or *so as to* negative, we put *not* before *to*.**

*Please speak quietly **in order not to disturb** other users of the library.*
*Please turn off your cell phones **so as not to ruin** the movie for other people.*

so and *such*

1 **We can use *so* or *such* to emphasize adjectives, adverbs, nouns, and noun phrases.**

*That's **so expensive**!*
*You walk **so quickly**!*
*He's **such a fool**.*
*It's **such an interesting place to visit**.*

2 **We also use *so / such* to show how one thing is the result of another. We use *so* with adjectives and adverbs, and *such (a)* with nouns.**

*It was **so expensive** that I couldn't afford to buy it.*
*You walk **so quickly** that I can't keep up with you.*
*He's **such a fool** that I avoid talking to him.*

3 **We connect the ideas with the word *that*, but it can be left out.**

*The book was so boring (**that**) I didn't finish it.*

UNIT 12

Phrasal verbs

A phrasal verb is a combination of a verb with a preposition or an adverb – this creates a new verb that often has a meaning that is completely different from the verb alone. For example, the verb "take" means "get" or "obtain," and "part" means "a section of something," but the phrasal verb "take part in" means "to participate in something." Phrasal verbs are very frequent in both spoken and written English.

1 **Most phrasal verbs have two parts.**

*I can't **work out** the answer. (find by thinking)*
*I didn't **take part in** the celebration. (participate)*

2 **With some phrasal verbs, the two parts can be separated by the object of the verb.**

*I **worked out** the answer.* OR *I **worked** the answer **out**.*

However, when the object is a pronoun, it must come between the two parts.

*I worked **it** out.* (NOT ~~*I worked out it.*~~)

3 **In other phrasal verbs, these parts can never be separated.**

*We **took part in** the celebration.*
(NOT ~~*I took part the celebration in.*~~)

4 **To find out if a phrasal verb can be split or not, look in a dictionary.**

If it can be split, it will be listed: work st out.
If it can't be split, it will be listed: take part in st.

5 **Some phrasal verbs have more than one meaning.**

*My car's **broken down**. (stopped working)*
*When she heard the news, she **broke down**. (started crying)*

I wish / If only + past perfect

We use *I wish* or *If only* + past perfect to express regret about past actions or events.

***I wish I'd been nice** to her. (= I wasn't nice to her, and I am sorry about it.)*
***I wish** you **hadn't opened** it. (= You opened it, and I am sorry about it.)*
***If only I'd listened** to my parents. (= I didn't listen to them, and I regret it.)*
***If only** we **hadn't missed** the bus. (= We missed the bus, and I regret it.)*

IRREGULAR VERBS

Base form	Simple past	Past participle
be	was / were	been
beat	beat	beaten
become	became	become
begin	began	begun
bite	bit	bitten
blow	blew	blown
break	broke	broken
breed	bred	bred
bring	brought	brought
build	built	built
burn	burned	burned
buy	bought	bought
can	could	–
catch	caught	caught
choose	chose	chosen
come	came	come
cost	cost	cost
cut	cut	cut
do	did	done
draw	drew	drawn
dream	dreamed	dreamed
drink	drank	drunk
drive	drove	driven
eat	ate	eaten
fall	fell	fallen
feel	felt	felt
fight	fought	fought
find	found	found
flee	fled	fled
fly	flew	flown
forget	forgot	forgotten
forgive	forgave	forgiven
freeze	froze	frozen
get	got	gotten
give	gave	given
go	went	gone
grow	grew	grown
hang	hung	hung
have	had	had
hear	heard	heard
hide	hid	hidden
hit	hit	hit
hold	held	held
hurt	hurt	hurt
keep	kept	kept
know	knew	known
lay	laid	laid
lead	led	led
learn	learned	learned
leave	left	left

Base form	Simple past	Past participle
lend	lent	lent
let	let	let
lie	lay	lain
light	lit	lit
lose	lost	lost
make	made	made
mean	meant	meant
meet	met	met
pay	paid	paid
put	put	put
quit	quit	quit
read	read	read
ride	rode	ridden
ring	rang	rung
rise	rose	risen
run	ran	run
say	said	said
see	saw	seen
seek	sought	sought
sell	sold	sold
send	sent	sent
set	set	set
shake	shook	shaken
shoot	shot	shot
show	showed	shown
shut	shut	shut
sing	sang	sung
sink	sank	sunk
sit	sat	sat
sleep	slept	slept
speak	spoke	spoken
spend	spent	spent
spill	spilled	spilled
spread	spread	spread
stand	stood	stood
steal	stole	stolen
stick	stuck	stuck
strike	struck	struck
swim	swam	swum
swing	swung	swung
take	took	taken
teach	taught	taught
tell	told	told
think	thought	thought
throw	threw	thrown
understand	understood	understood
wake	woke	woken
wear	wore	worn
win	won	won
write	wrote	written

ACKNOWLEDGEMENTS

The authors and publishers acknowledge the following sources of copyright material and are grateful for the permissions granted. While every effort has been made, it has not always been possible to identify the sources of all the material used, or to trace all copyright holders. If any omissions are brought to our notice, we will be happy to include the appropriate acknowledgements on reprinting and in the next update to the digital edition, as applicable.

Key: U = Unit, WU = Welcome Unit.

Text

U12: Text from *Bullring Kid and Country Cowboy Level 4 Intermediate* by Louise Clover, Cambridge English: Towards FCE. Copyright © Cambridge University Press – All rights reserved.

Photographs

The following photographs are sourced from Getty Images.

U7: FatCamera/E+; LRArmstrong/iStock/Getty Images Plus; Nick Dale/Design Pics; **U8**: Qi Yang/Moment; Luis Diaz Devesa/Moment; tane-mahuta/iStock/Getty Images Plus; andresr/E+; Bryan Mullennix/EyeEm; **U9**: JohnnyGreig/E+; Glowimages; Naomi Rahim/Moment; Marco Simoni/Cultura; **U10**: monkeybusinessimages/iStock/Getty Images Plus; chee gin tan/E+; JazzIRT/E+; **U11**: Martin Harvey/The Image Bank; **U12**: bymuratdeniz/E+; Bettmann; Bruce Glikas/FilmMagic; Juanmonino/E+.

Cover photography by Mustafagull/E+/Getty Images; George Pachantouris/Moment/Getty Images.

Illustrations

U7: Mark Ruffle; Martin Sanders; **U8**: Daniela Geremia; **U10**: Adam Linley; **U12**: Ben Scruton; Daniela Geremia.

Video Stills

Video production by Silversun.

Audio Production by CityVox, New York.